10 STEPS
to
VENTURE SUCCESS

Starting and Succeeding
in
Your Own Business

A Business Development Workbook

Dr. William R. Osgood

A Knowledge Institute, Inc. Publication

10 Steps to Venture Success
A Learning System for Business Owners, Managers, and the Self-Employed

Copyright (c) by Dr. William R. Osgood 2009, 2nd Edition 2011
ISBN: 978-1-935988-18-2

This publication is designed to provide accurate and authoritative information in regard to the subject matter covered. It is sold with the understanding that the publisher is not engaged in rendering legal, accounting, or other professional service. If legal advice or other expert assistance is required, the services of a competent professional person should be sought.

> — from a declaration of principles jointly adopted by a committee of the American Bar Association and a committee of publishers

The Knowledge Institute is a leading academic institution and think tank that specializes in self-employment and entrepreneurial education. Through multiple forms of public/private collaboration and direct services, the Knowledge Institute has helped millions of individuals globally to start, grow and succeed in business. Products and services include curriculum development, eLearning, individual and group facilitation, publishing, virtual business learning community design and content development, and consulting.

As both scholars and practitioners in the field of entrepreneurship, Knowledge Institute founders are recognized as innovators in multimedia and interactive learning systems by the U.S. Small Business Administration, Fortune 500 companies and leading federal and state small business development agencies.

Please direct comments, questions or suggestions regarding this publication to Knowledge Institute Editorial Department, at the address below:

Knowledge Institute, Inc.
11 Court Street, Suite 230
Exeter, New Hampshire 03833 USA
(603) 658-0340, fax (603) 658-0343
www.bdki.com

Printed in the United States of America

Dr. Bill's
Rules of the Road
for
Small Business Success

1. Talk is cheap – Planning without action is a waste of time

2. Not everyone is suited to starting and managing their own business

3. Business feasibility analysis and plan development follow a very well defined process that is grounded in common sense – it is not rocket science

4. If these rules are not respected and followed, the new venture will almost certainly fail

5. If there are no customers, there is no business

6. Breakeven is an essential concept for every venture that has any overhead or fixed costs

7. Breakeven can be understood by anyone

8. Cost and revenue projections are not simply a fantasy

9. Cash flow is king

10. The fairy godmother will not show-up

Table of Contents

Step 6: Forecasting

Step 7: Financing

Step 8: Resource Networks

Step 9: Business Launch

Step 10: Monitor Progress

About the Knowledge Institute

The Knowledge Institute is a leading academic institution and think tank that specializes in self-employment and entrepreneurial education. Through multiple forms of public/private collaboration and direct services, the Knowledge Institute has helped millions of individuals globally to start, grow and succeed in business.

Products and services include curriculum development, eLearning, individual and group facilitation, publishing, virtual business learning community design, content development, and consulting. Clients include government agencies, nonprofit organizations, Fortune 500 companies, academic institutions and individuals.

Recognized as innovators in multimedia and interactive learning systems, Knowledge Institute founders are both scholars and practitioners in the field of entrepreneurship. Dr. Deborah Osgood is the creator and chief architect of multiple virtual business learning communities and author of *An Entrepreneurial Systems Approach to Dropout Prevention: A Student-Centric Approach to Academic Engagement*, and *Who Am I? A Guide to Self-Discovery and Self-Employment*. Dr. William Osgood has written over 25 business management books published in multiple languages and distributed internationally. Both Deborah and William have succeeded in multiple business ventures and are experts in entrepreneurial education, program design and implementation.

Other publications of the Knowledge Institute include:

- 5 Steps to Successful Self-Employment
- Panic, People & Process – An Entrepreneurial Development Handbook from start-up to high growth
- The Business Planning Guide
- The Strategic Management Learning Series – 12 "How-To" workbooks, supporting the management of smaller enterprises:
    - Cash Flow
    - Forecasting
    - Management Control
    - Target Marketing
    - Time Management

- o Financing
- o Human Resource Management
- o Inventory Control
- o Marketing Communications
- o Credit & Collections
- o Strategic Analysis
- o Knowledge Management Systems

Online Interactive Learning Systems

10 Steps to Venture Success is also available online as an interactive Self-paced learning program. Course Content walks participants through a seamless and comprehensive process for assessing their business skills, validating their business ideas, compiling a development strategy and launching a new business. Interactive Features offer step-by-step exercises, customizable worksheets, sales forecasting templates, documented results and measurable outcomes - all while learning at their own pace. Learning Options permit working with a volunteer business mentor at no additional cost, or a professional consultant via email or telephone at an additional fixed rate. Upon completion, users receive a Certificate of Achievement.

For more information, go to *www.BDKI.com*. For publications, click on *Bookstore*, for online learning programs, click on *eLearning*.

Contact:

Knowledge Institute
11 Court Street, Suite 230
Exeter, NH 03833
603-658-0340
info@bdki.com

10

Steps to
Venture Success

Dr. William R. Osgood

10 Steps to Venture Success

What If?

> What if I could start my own retail business?
> What if I could be a communication consultant?
> What if I could launch my own computer service company?
> What if I could succeed at running my own franchise venture?
> What if I could make money running a fitness center?
> What if I could talk to someone about my business ideas?

What if there were no limits to your ideas and dreams? What if there was a way for you to participate in an innovative program where you could test out your ideas for being your own boss and making money selling your own products, services, talents or inventions? What if you could connect with an experienced business advisor who could respond to your questions and help guide your business development efforts?

Why Not?

Read on to discover how this workbook provides a thorough, step-by-step framework for developing business skills, knowledge and a support network for successfully launching your own business.

By the end of the workbook you will have put together most of the components that you'll need to actually start your own business!

THE SKY IS NOT THE LIMIT

Welcome. . .

Getting Started

By utilizing this workbook, you are already taking the first step of what is an exciting and rewarding adventure for many. For others, starting and running their own venture is a bad choice. The reality is that most businesses will be out of business in less than 5 years after they get started – and most of these because they failed. The sad truth of the matter is that most of these business failures can be avoided. That is the purpose of this workbook – to help you avoid the pitfalls that can limit a business's success or even make it fail, and reinforce the strengths and decisions that can lead to success.

Following the 10 Step program is an important activity

Set aside the time

You'll need the time to think about your answers

The program is a methodical 10-step process that begins with a self-assessment of suitability for being in business, and concludes with a blueprint for implementing the new business venture.

Each component of the program introduces a critical aspect of the entrepreneurial process and provides instructional and background material followed by self-testing tools to allow you to assess your own skills relative to the key issues of that course component. This interactive feature will productively lead you through the venture planning and preparation process.

Each step of the program builds on the prior step. At every stage, we introduce the issues that need to be addressed, the questions that need to be answered, and the additional resources that are available to assist with supporting a successful business venture. The program is self-paced – you proceed to the next session when you are ready.

It is critical to spend time with the exercises. They are designed to provoke your thinking and the answers may not be immediately evident. We encourage you to read the materials presented thoughtfully. For once, there are no predetermined right or wrong answers – the right answers are the ones that work for you.

Using the Worksheets

The worksheets provide a frame of reference by allowing you to compare yourself against various historic industry benchmarks

These benchmarks are decision tools – not the answers

You decide what makes sense – for you

The worksheets are in an interactive format. They are set up here to be completed manually and scored. If you are working on a computer, you can complete the worksheet and then e-mail it to yourself (and anyone else you feel might be interested – your friend, counselor / consultant, or spouse for example).

We encourage you to set up a folder so that you can archive these forms once you have them completed and printed. In this manner, you will have a hard copy of your hard work throughout the program, and a valuable source of reference as you move forward.

It is valuable to have someone to discuss the various worksheet results with. There are really no right or wrong answers – instead, the right answer is the one that makes most sense for you. That is why using someone else as a sounding board can help determine whether it all really makes good sense.

If you are not already working with a local business counselor or adviser such as a Small Business Development Center, Women's Business Center, or SCORE, visit *www.BUZGate.org* to find an experienced virtual business mentor. The *BUZGate* website will also provide you with a range of additional free resources based on your own interests, including young entrepreneurs, veterans, women, minorities, and manufacturers.

In addition to encouraging you to work with an experienced business mentor, this 10 Step Program will introduce you to a variety of other local business assistance agencies that offer free and low-cost help in practically all areas of business management including import/export, funding, marketing, site location, workforce development and government contracting. These are listed in *BUZGate* as well. You will find many references to the BUZGate Resource Community throughout this Workbook – take advantage of these resources – our tax dollars pay for these programs and as a result, they are free to users.

Contact these resource providers to not only gain more insight and skills based on your own particular entrepreneurial needs and interests, but to also begin building your support network for the longer term. Leverage the knowledge and wisdom of others – Common Sense!

How to Proceed

o Read the text

o Keep paper and pen handy to jot down ideas as you read

o Do the exercises – thoughtfully – allow sufficient time to really think about your answers

o Find someone to discuss you responses with – a spouse, partner, mentor or counselor – it's not really about their opinion, rather it is the process of discussing your ideas that helps shape their validity.

o Follow the links to the resources listed – build your networks

About the Bonus Material

We have included much valuable information at the end of the Workbook that can supplement your direct work in completing the 10 Steps.

o Five Steps to Effective Problem Solving is a methodical way to approach solving any business or any other problem. We almost always sub-optimize because our thinking is constrained by the limitations we believe are inherent in the situation. The approach presented here first allows a much broader view of problem identification, then allows you to identify a much broader range of alternatives than you would normally consider. Our advice – study this approach, and start to use it every time you need to make a decision about anything!

o Eupsychian Systems Analysis (ESA) is a process of optimized goal setting. How can you know if your business is doing as well as possible? For most businesses, goal setting consists of defining targets relative to where the business has been: "We want to do 15% better than last year." What kind of a goal is this anyway? How do we know that last years level of activity was actually OK? How do we know that 15% more this year is OK – or even possible? This kind of marginal goal setting is generally an ineffective process and one that is almost guaranteed to be suboptimal. ESA helps to define the most optimal targets. It provides a framework useful in modifying idealized, optimized goals within the reality of a given environment. Once goals are made both optimal and realistic, they become achievable. ESA is designed for problem solving involving multidimensional and interdependent subsystems in any setting, and is especially appropriate for use where the issues may not be so clear cut or obvious.

o Tactical Evaluation Process is a highly structured way to develop an analysis of your overall business situation. It is called Tactical because it is about developing tactics to optimize your business outcomes. It is a valuable process to apply to an existing business as you try to come to grips with the various issues at play. It is also a valuable approach to evaluate the business strategy you will develop through the 10 Steps in this book.

o Using SWOT Analysis to Improve Your Business is a problem-solving approach you can use to productively engage others in your business to benefit from their insights, and to allow them to become more involved in the operation. There is a very specific process to follow to achieve the most productive results. A form is included for you to print-out and use with your partner, spouse, or key employees.

The 10 Step Program

The *10 Steps to Venture Success* program is comprised of 10 sections, each designed to support you in productively addressing the following entrepreneurial components:

Step 1: Self-Assessment
Am I suited for running my own business?

Step 2: Business Idea
Do I have a viable business idea?

Step 3: Market Analysis
Is there a market for my business idea?

Step 4: Management Skills
Do I have the skills needed to make this work?

Step 5: Business Plan
Do I have a complete business plan?

Step 6: Forecasting
Do I have a realistic forecast of revenues and costs?

Step 7: Financing
Am I aware of my business financing needs?

Step 8: Outside Resources
Do I understand what assistance may be available from public agencies?

Step 9: Venture Launch
Do I have the licenses, approvals and other issues covered that are needed for actually starting the new business?

Step 10: Monitor Progress
Am I prepared to monitor and control operations once started?

Outcomes

By following the program systematically and completely, a great deal of confusion about what to do next will be eliminated and the chances of your business success will be greatly increased.

Good Luck as you start on this exciting adventure!!

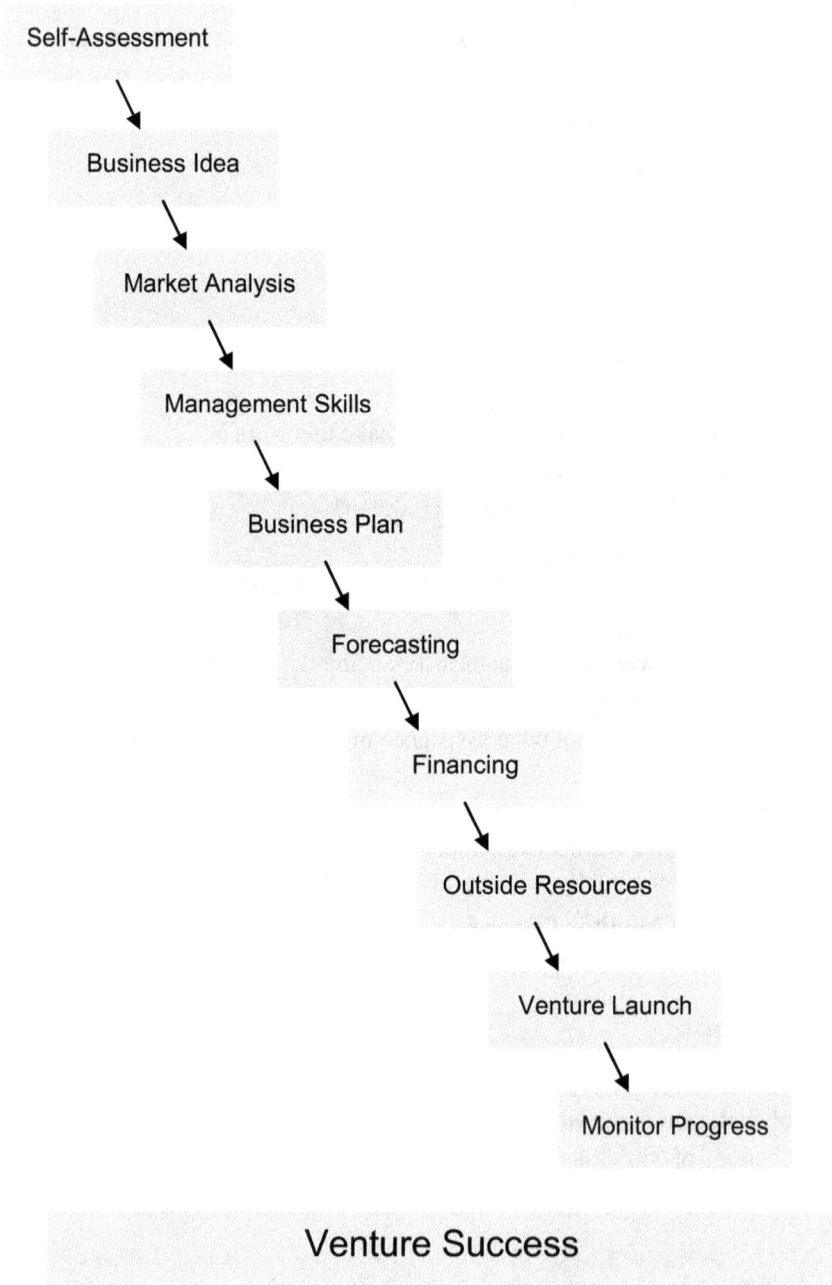

Self-Assessment

Business Idea

Market Analysis

Management Skills

Business Plan

Forecasting

Financing

Outside Resources

Venture Launch

Monitor Progress

Venture Success

1

STEP 1

Self-
Assessment

Am I suited for running my own business?

In this Section:

- o Introduction
  - o Should you be in business for yourself?
  - o Pros & Cons
  - o What it takes
- o Exercises:
  - o 10 Great Reasons to Be in Business for Yourself
  - o 10 Great Reasons NOT To Be In Business for Yourself
  - o Common Entrepreneurial Traits
  - o Common Mistakes That Lead to Business Failure
  - o Entrepreneurial Aptitude Index
  - o Summary

Step 1

Self-Assessment

Introduction

So you think you might want to be in business for yourself.

For many people, this is a personally rewarding and financially profitable journey. For others, the challenges associated with identifying a viable business idea, developing a market strategy, and managing a profitable operation over time may be too overwhelming. By following the self-assessment process presented here, these and other issues associated with undertaking your own venture will be productively addressed.

There are five parts to this session. The first four worksheets set the stage for you to self-evaluate against different benchmarks that have proven to be important for business success. The last part links to a scored self-assessment quiz.

Good Idea

Find a business mentor, counselor or advisor to discuss these exercises with – having outside objectivity is priceless!

While none of these activities will give you an absolute answer about whether or not you should start your own business, they do provide very useful insights, and so represent a valuable way to get started.

First, look at the pros and cons of being in business. The pros are outlined in the *10 Great Reasons to Be In Business for Yourself*. The cons are outlined in the *10 Great Reasons Not to Be In Business for Yourself*. The best way to do this is to copy or print out both of the exercises, place them side-by-side, then look at the differences and determine which are most important to you.

Once you have reviewed these pros and cons, take a look at the characteristics of people who have succeeded as entrepreneurs, and think about how you stack-up against this list.

There is a list of common mistakes that often lead to business failure. Look at this list and try to determine what you can do to avoid these same problems.

Now, take the *Self Assessment/Risk Assessment Exercises*. It is essential that you are as honest as possible here – your future security and happiness depends on you making the best decisions possible. You will calculate a numerical score for the exercises that will help indicate your own suitability for the demands that lie ahead, or show areas you will need to compensate for that could prove to be limitations further on.

If it turns out that you are not suited for running your own business, better that you learn it now, than through the business failure that will almost certainly follow.

Your Success Is In Your Own Hands

Exercises Step 1: Self-Assessment

1a. 10 Great Reasons To Be In Business for Yourself

1b. 10 Great Reasons NOT To Be In Business for Yourself

1c. Common Entrepreneurial Traits

1d. Common Mistakes That Lead to Business Failure

1e. Entrepreneurial Aptitude Index

1f. Summary

Now on to the exercises....

1a: 10 Great Reasons to Be In Business for Yourself

Below are some of the attitudes and desires that many successful entrepreneurs possess. Read the list carefully. Think about how each of the statements relate to you – your ideas, desires, motivations, and areas of comfort or discomfort. In this exercise, quickly check each category with the answer that best relates to you, then go back and think about each – perhaps you might change your mind with this further refection – you can always come back later and change your answer.

Using the rating scale, place an X in the Column you relate to best:

Column a: Strongly Agree
Column b: Agree
Column c: Neutral
Column d: Disagree
Column e: Strongly

10 Great Reasons to Be In Business For Yourself	Column				
	a	b	c	d	e
1. Be your own boss					
2. Ability to set your own hours and working conditions					
3. Hard work directly benefits you and your business					
4. Undertaking an exciting new venture					
5. Control over earning and growth potential					
6. Unlimited opportunities to challenge yourself and learn					
7. Chance to be creative and take risks					
8. Ability to fully use your skills, knowledge and talent					
9. Financial independence					
10. Ability to work in the industry / field of your choice					
Total Each Column					
Multiply By	5	4	3	2	1
Total Value Each Column					
Total Score (Sum all Columns)					

```
                    INTERPRETATION
        Score of 34-50:   High Match
        Score of 21-35:   Medium Match
        Score of  0-20:   Low Match
```

1b: 10 Great Reasons NOT to Be In Business for Yourself

Not everyone is suited to start and run his or her own business operation. Think about the following list of reasons not to be in business and see how they might match-up with concerns or issues that you may be facing. If some of these match reasons you face, you should begin to question whether you should proceed with the goal of going into business. Read this list carefully, complete the form, and be as honest with yourself as possible when checking off which level of response you can best identify with.

Using the rating scale, place an X in the Column you relate to best:

Column a: Strongly Agree
Column b: Agree
Column c: Neutral
Column d: Disagree
Column e: Strongly Disagree

10 Great Reasons NOT to Be In Business For Yourself	Column				
	a	b	c	d	e
1. Long hours which can include nights, weekends, and holidays					
2. Hard work					
3. High stress and emotional strain					
4. Financial risk					
5. Potential for unstable income and loss of benefits					
6. Lower quality of life until your business is established					
7. Complete responsibility for all aspects of the business operation					
8. Need to have many different skills and talents					
9. Potential for business failure					
10. Social isolation					
Total Each Column					
Multiply By	5	4	3	2	1
Total Value Each Column					
Total Score (Sum all Columns)					

```
            INTERPRETATION

Score of 34-50:   High Match

Score of 21-35:   Medium Match

Score of  0-20:   Low Match
```

17

1c: Common Entrepreneurial Traits

Individuals who have succeeded in starting and operating their own business organizations have certain characteristics in common. On the next page is a list of the most common characteristics in this regard.

This list is valuable as a basis for you to compare yourself to and determine how closely you match up with these characteristics. Its not a problem if you don't match on all of them, but where you may be missing in the match should give you cause for further thought to see how this might affect your own chances for success.

Review this list and talk it over with someone else – your partner, mentor or counselor. Using this as a basis for discussion can often uncover other issues affecting the business development process. Read this list carefully, complete the form, and be as honest with yourself as possible when checking off which level of response you can best identify with.

By adding up the numbers you have checked, you can rate yourself.

Using the rating scale, place an X in the Column you relate to best.

Column a: Strongly Agree
Column b: Agree
Column c: Neutral
Column d: Disagree
Column e: Strongly Disagree

Common Entrepreneurial Traits	Column				
	a	b	c	d	e
1. Able to tolerate failure					
2. Committed					
3. Competitive					
4. Creative					
5. Hard Worker					
6. High Energy					
7. Independent					
8. Innovative					
9. Inquisitive					
10. Persistent					
11. Problem Solver					
12. Risk Taker					
13. Self-confident					
14. Strong Desire to Succeed					
15. Strong Organizational Skills					
Total Each Column					
Multiply By	5	4	3	2	1
Total Value Each Column					
Total Score (Sum All Columns)					

INTERPRETATION

Score of 51-75: High Match

Score of 26-50: Medium Match

Score of 0-25: Low Match

1d: Common Mistakes That Lead To Business Failure

It may be surprising to learn that businesses in totally different industries, of totally different sizes, and with totally different resource capacities fail for many of the same reasons. On the next page is a list of some of the more common pitfalls.

Review this list and talk it over with someone else – your partner, mentor or counselor. Using this as a basis for discussion can often uncover other issues affecting the business development process. Read this list carefully, complete the form, and be as honest with yourself as possible when checking off which level of response you can best identify with.

By adding up the numbers you have checked, you can rate yourself.

Using the rating scale, place an X in the Column you relate to best.

Column a: Can Avoid

Column b: Concerned About

Column c: Don't Understand (Need to research)

Common Entrepreneurial Mistakes	Column		
	a	b	c
1. Failure to develop a sound business plan			
2. Failure to attract and retain customers			
3. Failure to develop marketing niches			
4. Failure to maintain self-sufficient cash flow			
5. Failure to control costs			
6. Failure to identify problems early-on			
7. Failure to select appropriate resource people and staff			
8. Failure to forecast growth cycle of new products/services			
9. Failure to innovate			
10. Failure to monitor and respond to trends			
11. Failure to use technology			
12. Failure to adjust to changing markets and competition			
13. Failure to use the Internet			
14. Failure to maintain control			
15. Failure to work-through family problems			
16. Failure to manage inventory			
17. Failure to generate new and retain existing customers			
18. Failure to deal with impending litigation			
19. Failure to obtain needed financial resources			
20. Failure to file IRS documents			
21. Failure to communicate internally			
22. Failure to keep good records			
Total Each Column			
Multiply By	3	2	1
Total Value Each Column			
Total Score (Sum All Columns)			

```
.......................................................
:                INTERPRETATION                      :
:  Score of 45-66:  Well Prepared                    :
:  Score of 23-44:  Be Concerned                     :
:  Score of  0-22:  Need To Learn More               :
.......................................................
```

1e: Entrepreneurial Aptitude Index

This Entrepreneurial Aptitude Assessment presents various behavioral traits that may contribute to being successful in starting and operating your own venture, and shows the result as a quantitative score. This score can help reinforce the conclusions you have been reaching in the prior exercises. On the next page is a list of some of the more common behavioral traits.

Review this list and talk it over with someone else – your partner, mentor or counselor. Using this as a basis for discussion can often uncover other issues affecting the business development process.

Read this list carefully, complete the form, and be as honest with yourself as possible when checking off which level of response you can best identify with.

Using the rating scale, place an X in the Column you relate to best.

Column a: Strongly Agree
Column b: Agree
Column c: Neutral
Column d: Disagree
Column e: Strongly Disagree

Entrepreneurial Aptitude Index	Column				
	a	b	c	d	e
1. Succeeding is very important to me					
2. Once I set a goal, I see it through					
3. I am self-confident					
4. I do not like being told what to do					
5. I am determined					
6. I will take a chance when I think the idea has promise					
7. I like being in charge					
8. I enjoy continually learning new things					
9. When I set my mind on something, I am persistent					
10. I am inventive					
11. I consider the cup half full, not half empty					
12. I don't get tired easily when I am interested in a project					
13. I am a risk-taker					
14. Others have called me hardheaded					
15. I would like to set my own hours and working conditions					
16. I prefer my own way of doing things					
17. I see emotional challenges as opportunities for personal growth					
18. I work well by myself					
19. I view problems as obstacles to overcome					
20. I prefer thinking out of the box and being innovative					
21. I am flexible					
22. I enjoy figuring things out					
23. I often trust my instincts					
24. I want to have control over my earning and growth potential					
25. I view mistakes as missed opportunities					
Total Each Column					
Multiply By	5	4	3	2	1
Total Value Each Column					
Total Score (Sum All Columns)					

INTERPRETATION

Score of 86-125: High Match

Score of 46-85: Medium Match

Score of 0-45: Low Match

Find Free Help

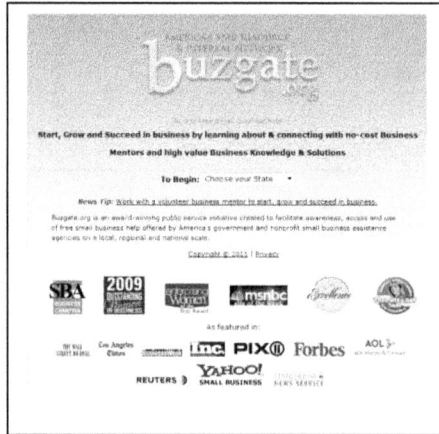

www.BUZGate.org

BUZGate is a state-by-state entrepreneurial education community and resource directory cataloging government and nonprofit agency programs tailored to supporting small business start-up, growth and sustainability. Programs include help with:

Advocacy	Funding	Taxes
Business Research	Import/Export	Training
Counseling	Marketing	Veterans in Business
Credentialing	Networking	Women in Business
Disadvantaged	Regulatory Issues	Workforce
Economic	Site Finding	Development
Development	Start-up	Youth in Business
Financing	Statistical Data	...and more

Summary Step 1

Undertaking your own business venture can be exciting, rewarding and profitable, but it is critical that you first conclude that it is the right course of action for you – and only you can ultimately form this conclusion.

Each of the assessment tools presented in this first Step of the *10 Steps to Venture Success* has been designed to help you look at the issues of self-employment and entrepreneurship from different perspectives. Now take a look at what the exercises are suggesting so far.

Instructions: Enter you score from each of the worksheets in this Step.

Worksheet Summary	Your Score
1a. 10 Great Reasons To Be In Business for Yourself	
1b. 10 Great Reasons NOT To Be In Business for Yourself	
1c. Common Entrepreneurial Traits	
1d. Common Mistakes That Lead To Business Failure	
1e. Self Assessment/Risk Assessment Quiz	
Total of All Scores	

If you scored above 245, you show a strong aptitude for entrepreneurship.

If you scored between 120 and 244, you have potential but may want to improve skills in weaker areas by seeking training or hiring someone with needed skills.

If you scored between 110 and 119, you may not want to start a business alone. You may want to look for a business partner who can compliment you in the areas where you are weak. Keep in mind that having a partner can bring with it difficulties you may not want to experience as well. Make such a decision carefully and for the right reasons.

If you scored below 109, operating your own business may not be for you. You will probably be happier and more successful working for someone else. However, only you can make that decision.

It is important to keep in mind that there are no definitive answers. This is just a tool. It is interesting to use and interpret, but you should keep it in perspective. The ultimate choice is yours.

2

STEP 2

Business Idea

Do I have a viable business idea?

In this Section:

- Introduction
  - Three Pitfalls
  - Business Idea Development
  - Business Idea Profile
  - Types of Business Opportunities
  - Starting Your Own Business
  - Buying a Franchise
  - Buying an Existing Business
- Exercises:
  - Personal Preferences Inventory
  - Personal Skills Inventory
  - Business Idea Options
  - Business Idea Profile
  - Summary

Step 2

Business Idea

Introduction

In order to have a business, you must first have a business idea.

Some of the most successful businesses come from an individual's ability to turn a hobby or passionate interest into a revenue generating operation. Identifying what you like, where you believe your skills or talents are strong, and then determining if there is a market for the resulting product or service is the essence of coming up with a viable business idea. This step and the next will guide you through this process.

The best place to start this step is with reviewing mistakes that people often make in choosing a business idea. Being aware of mistakes others have made will help keep you from making them for yourself. Some common pitfalls to watch out for:

Pitfall # 1 Rushing to make a decision	Your success will depend on the business idea you choose. Take your time to consider your options and explore your ideas – you may not get a second chance.
Pitfall # 2 Turning a hobby into a business without doing your homework	Building a business around your hobbies or interests can be a great idea, but there must be sufficient demand for the product or service or the business will not succeed.

Pitfall # 3

Not asking for help

There are many resources available that can serve as a sounding board for you to bounce business ideas off and to learn from.

Be willing to test your idea on others and listen to their feedback; it will help you to further refine your business idea.

This Step is divided into three categories:

1. Business Idea Development

2. Business Idea Profile

3. Types of Business Opportunities

There are a series of worksheets to help you organize your thoughts, and some information regarding different types of business opportunities:

1. Starting Your Own Business

2. Buying a Franchise

3. Buying an Existing Business

These are followed by a series of links to other sources for business ideas.

Action

Once you have completed the worksheets and reviewed all of the materials, there is a final worksheet in this step to help you begin to describe your idea. Make sure that you do not miss this final worksheet, as it will be critical to other sections later on.

Exercises Step 2: Business Idea

2a. Personal Preferences Inventory

2b. Personal Skills Inventory

2c. Business Idea Options

2d. Business Idea Profile

2e. Summary

Now on to the exercises….

2a: Personal Preferences Inventory

The logical first steps for developing a business idea are to conduct a personal preferences inventory and a personal skills inventory. The more nearly the business matches with your interests and strengths, the more likely you are to be happy in the operation, which is usually a strong additional impetus for success.

For the Personal Preferences Inventory Worksheet, look at your hobbies, volunteer experience, and leisure activities. What do you like to do? What don't you like to do? What interests you? What makes you happy? With the necessary business knowledge, something you take pleasure in doing could be a viable business idea for you. Use the following worksheet to start organizing your ideas.

Read this list carefully, complete the form, and be as honest with yourself as possible. Your answers will help to identify potential business ideas. Once completed, review this list and talk it over with someone else – your partner, mentor or counselor. Using this as a basis for discussion can often uncover other issues affecting the business development process.

Personal Preferences Inventory
a. List below some of your preferred activities
1.   Hobbies
2.   Special Interests
3.   Volunteer Work
4.   Leisure Pursuits
5.   Other Activities

Personal Preferences Inventory (Continued)
b. With reference to the prior categories, respond to the questions below
1.   What aspects of these activities do you like the most? Why?
2.   What aspects of these activities do you like the least? Why?
3.   What types of activities do you consider t be a lot of fun? Why?
4.   What courses or subjects did you like to study in school? Why?
5.   Have you had any jobs that you really enjoyed? What did you like about the job?
6.   What are some of the achievements you are most proud of? Why?
7.   If you could do anything as your own business, what would it be?

2b: Personal Skills Inventory

The next step in developing your business idea is to conduct a personal skills inventory. Here you can list areas of your personal background, such as any special training, skills, education, and job experiences that you have. What do you already know how to do? Could you do any of your past jobs by working for yourself? What past responsibilities have you had? What tasks are you comfortable completing? What are you skilled at? What can you offer to customers that other businesses are not currently offering?

Read this list carefully, complete the form, and be as honest with yourself as possible. Your answers will help to identify potential business ideas. Once completed, review this list and talk it over with someone else – your partner, mentor or counselor. Using this as a basis for discussion can often uncover other issues affecting the business development process.

Personal Skills Inventory
a. List below skills you have acquired through your various activities
1. Educational Background
2. Special Training Received
3. Work/Career Experiences
4. Sports Activities or Recreation
5. Other Skills Acquired

Personal Skills Inventory (Continued)
b. With reference to the prior categories, respond to the questions below
1.   What are some of the areas where you are most skilled? What do you already know how to do?
2.   Which of the skills do you take the most pleasure in using? Why?
3.   What industries or businesses do you have experience in?
4.   What responsibilities, tasks, or duties have you had in the past? Would you want to do these things as a part of your own business?
5.   Are there ways that your current skills, training, experience, or education could improve upon an existing product, process or business idea?
6.   What could you offer to customers that other businesses are not currently offering?

2c: Business Idea Options

In addition to the exercises you have just completed, there are a myriad of places to find good business ideas that may match with your interests and skills.

An idea does not have to be novel or even original; in fact very few businesses are based on original ideas. Look around, watch the news, talk to friends and family, observe things around you, and think about how you can translate them into a business idea. Many times growth of an area creates the need for additional providers of standard products or services. You can also look at business areas that need improvement. Think about the products and services you use or that you've heard other people talk about. Are there any that could be improved on? Is there anything they're not offering that would be of value? Consider starting a business that fills a need that isn't being met by the current providers. Focus on a niche. Many businesses have failed by trying to be all things to all people. Try to identify a niche that you would enjoy working in and build your business idea around it. There are many sources for business ideas and opportunities.

Following are some valuable links to get you started:

Useful Resources

- o Business Ideas from www.bizbuysell.com and the Wall Street Journal

- o Business Franchise Advisors from www.FranNet.com

- o Government Contracting Ideas from https://www.fbo.gov/index?cck=1&au=&ck=

- o Online search for business opportunities – but beware of scams

As you begin to narrow-in on your idea, it is essential to get it down in writing. The exercise on the next page will help you start to get your ideas organized.

2c. Business Idea Options

List some ideas you learned about that you think are interesting & why	
Business Idea	Why you think it is interesting for you

2d: Business Idea Profile

If you already have an idea for your business venture, write it down, and then list all the reasons you think it is a good idea, and one that you can make succeed. Just as you would consult a map to identify and plan the best route for a long journey, it is valuable to identify the core components or profile of your venture before you get started – for example, what resources will you require, why do you view the venture as viable, and who will buy what you are offering? These are just a few of the questions introduced below that will guide you in further profiling your business concept.

Think about your idea(s) for a business venture and answer the questions following to begin the development of an operational framework. If you do not know the answer, write down the best answer you can think of at this point in the development of your ideas – you can always come back later and change your answer – discuss the results with your mentor, counselor or partner.

Business Idea Profile
1. What is (will be) the business?
2. What type of business – retail, service, manufacturing?
3. What are the specific products/services that will be sold?
4. Why is your business going to be profitable?
5. List three reasons why you think that this is a good idea: a. b. c.

Business Idea Profile (Continued)

6. What market (customers) do you intend to serve? Where is the market located? How big is this market? What is your expected market share?

7. How will you get your products or services to this market? Or how will the market (customers) get to you?

8. Why you can serve this market better than your competition?

9. Why you have chosen your particular location?

10. Is there really a need for another business like the one you are planning to start?

11. What management and other personnel are available and required for the operation?

12. Why (if appropriate) will debt money or someone's equity investment make your business more profitable?

2e: Business Opportunity Alternatives

In addition to developing and pursuing your own business idea, you might also consider purchasing an existing business or a franchise license. Each of these choices has pros and cons to consider. The following outlines list some of these important considerations. There is not a worksheet in this section, but reading the material will provide valuable insights needed for the final worksheet in this session.

In this section

Starting your own business

Buying a franchise

Buying an existing business

1. Starting Your Own Business

When people start thinking about going into business, they typically think about starting from scratch. For many, and for good reasons, this may be the best idea. There are though, some downsides to this process as well. Here are both sides of the issue:

Pros

- o Freedom to mold the operation the way you want – It is your own business, built the way you feel it should be

- o Ability to create your own distinctive competitive advantage – You define the market for the new business, the marketing outreach tools, the reasons why you believe your potential customers would want to buy from you rather than from where ever they presently do business

- o Pride in creating something that has not existed before – Starting your own business and making it succeed is a unique personal achievement, and one that gives many business owners great satisfaction

o No carry-over baggage from some prior operations – You are not stuck with the accumulation of past operating decisions someone else has made and implemented, mistakes, employees, location, products, bad reputation or any other negative aspects

Cons

o Risk of failure is high for an unproven start-up – No matter how good you may think the idea, and no matter how well you may plan, there are no guarantees of success

o May be difficult to establish market, build a customer base – It is difficult at best to establish visibility for a new business; many operations compete for customer's attention and business

o Difficulty in securing suppliers – Suppliers may be unsure about the viability of a new operation, and may not want to take the risk that working with them could represent

o Must create facilities, equipment, operating systems from scratch - There is no proven business system; all of the parts must be understood, located, and assembled into an efficient effective operation

2. Buying A Franchise

If the thought of a pre-packaged business appeals to you, then you may want to consider buying a franchise. The US Small Business Administration defines franchising as "a legal and commercial relationship between the owner of a trademark, service mark, trade name, or advertising symbol and an individual or group wishing to use that identification in a business. The franchise governs the method of conducting business between the two parties. Generally, a franchisee sells goods or services supplied by the franchisor or that meet the franchisor's quality standards."

There are generally two types of franchise opportunities available. In product/trade name franchising, the franchise company owns the right to the name or trademark and sells that right to a franchisee. In business format franchising, the franchise company often provides an "out of the box business" with a full range of services, including site selection, training, product supply, marketing plans, and even financing assistance.

For more information on franchising visit the SBA's Consumer Guide to Buying a Franchise at http://www.sba.gov/content/franchising-overview For information on available franchising opportunities, please visit www.FranNet.com to connect with a professional counselor who will help you profile your desires and capabilities and then suggest opportunities that should be a valuable match.

There are both pros and cons for buying a franchise:

Pros

o   Proven business system – The franchisor has developed a methodology for running the business that can be followed, minimizing the need to develop such a system or learn by trial and error

o   Proven product / service – An opportunity to operate a business with wide market acceptance; you don't need to create this market reputation because it already exists

o   Marketing expertise – The franchisor has developed a proven marketing outreach program; you plug and play a system that will be successful in building your business

o   Financial assistance – Often the franchisor will help with arranging financing, both because they already have a reputation and because their franchisees often succeed

o   Professional guidance – The franchisor often has professional staff to provide guidance and share expertise that might otherwise simply not be available to a new business operation

o   Opportunity to learn – Even if you do not have experience in operating a particular type of business, you can learn what you need to know from the franchisor (MacDonald's operates Hamburger U)

o   Recognized standards – The franchisor typically provides quality standards to help assure that each operator will maintain the reputation for quality and service that makes the franchise valuable

o Efficiency – Because the business systems (and even physical assets) are already available, the business can often be started with less capital than might otherwise be required

Cons

o Cost of purchasing franchise – The franchisor is providing something of value; typically the franchisee is initially glad to pay for this value, but may become discouraged as time goes on and must still pay a royalty fee to the franchisor with less tangible assistance being provided

o Franchisor control – The same good news, a standard form of operation, can be the bad news as the franchisee must agree to follow the operational format and which typically will discourage adding other goods or services, promoting a different image, or changing other aspects of the operation

o Over-dependence or unsatisfied expectations – The franchisor cannot always know what is best for each local situation and so the franchisee must be prepared to make a certain level of decisions

o Risk of fraud or misunderstanding – There are unscrupulous franchisors that offer franchises that do not offer real value, or promises that are unrealistic

o Problems of termination or transfer – Because of the franchise agreement, it may be difficult to terminate at your choice, or the franchisor may have reserved the right to terminate against your will; also, the franchise agreement may prohibit the transfer of ownership if you want to sell the franchise or even if you die and hope that your heirs can inherit the business

o Poor performance of other franchisees – If other franchisees do not do a good job, the franchise can loose its reputation, and so could hurt your operation

3. Buying An Existing Business

If starting a business from the ground up is overwhelming or not appealing to you, consider buying a business that is already established. Business owners decide to sell their businesses for many reasons. Some owners are looking to retire while others wish to start new ventures. Whatever the reason, there are usually fully operational business available for sale and you may be able to purchase a business for less than it would cost to set up the business yourself, and save time and energy as well.

There are many sources for learning about business opportunities. The most popular are:

- o Business opportunity brokers
- o Classified newspaper ads
- o Companies that supply or set up new locations
- o Business opportunity trade shows

The US Small Business Administration refers to the following online resource guide from My Own Business for information on buying a business: http://www.myownbusiness.org/s10/index.html#1

There are both pros and cons for buying an already existing business:

Pros

- o Proven products, location, process, employees, market – The existing business is already in motion, and represents a proven viable operation
- o Planning can be based on historical data – Sales, costs, and growth trends are available through the past operating records of the business, and so do not represent speculation or guesswork
- o New owner benefits from experience of previous owner – The old owner may be willing to work with the new owner to pass along experience and help make a smooth transition for customers, employees, and suppliers

- o No start-up time required – The business is already in motion with an established market visibility and flow of sales revenues that help to reduce start-up costs

- o Employees and suppliers already in place – It is not necessary to recruit new employees and find out through trial and error whether they will work out; suppliers already have confidence in the existing operation and are likely to transfer that confidence to the new owner

- o Plant and equipment already established – Starting a new operation from scratch involves finding and assembling countless pieces; it is much easier and much less risky when they are already in place as a functioning system

- o May be available at a bargain price – There may be personal reasons why the old owner wants to sell; often because they want to retire or change their life style, or perhaps are even deceased. As well, they may have been such poor managers that the business is available through a bankruptcy sale

- o May facilitate securing financing – An existing operation is a proven operation through its history, or prior reputation for market and operations, and so may have greater credibility with a financing organization; the old owner may be willing to participate in the financing through holding a note for all or part of the selling price

Cons

- o Its someone else's idea and operation and may not fit with new owner's style, goals – The existing business is established with a certain personality and operational style that may not fit with the new owner

- o Previous owner may have created ill will – There may be a bad reputation with customers, suppliers, financiers which can be very difficult to overcome, no matter how the new owners may try to represent "Under new Ownership"

- o Change and innovation may be difficult to implement – The old business may have such a momentum that it is difficult to bring about change in the way it operates or reaches its customers

- o Location may now be suboptimal – Changes in transportation patterns or decline or change in population or neighborhoods may mean that the old location is no longer the best location; it can be expensive to move

- o Inventory may be old, obsolete – Part of the sale price of the business may include inventory that is no longer really marketable either because it is shop-worn or obsolete

- o May have poor employees – Employees may have a bad attitude because of past management styles, or may be so attached to the old owner that they do not want to accept the authority of the new owner

- o Facilities and equipment may be old, obsolete – Outdated facilities and equipment can represent a higher operating cost and/or a major expense to up-grade to current standards or to include labor or cost saving technologies

- o Could have supplier problems – Suppliers may have had a disagreement with the old owner, or a personal relationship that is not transferable to the new owner, or may not trust the new owner to be as effective as the old owner

- o Financing, legal issues – There may be legal issues with the IRS, impending customer law suits, or other problems the new owner will need to resolve

- o Business may be overpriced – The existing owners may have an inflated idea of what they think the business is really worth, particularly compared with the cost of starting a similar operation from scratch

Summary Step 2

In this Step, the goal is to define a business idea that meets your requirements, and appears to have prospects for success. These prospects will be further evaluated in later Steps.

Now, summarize your idea:

What is your business idea?

Why do you think it will work?

Now on to Step 3…

3

STEP 3

Market Research & Analysis

Is there a market for my business idea?

In this Section:

- o Introduction
- o Why Market Research
- o Sources of Market Data
- o Research References & Statistics
- o Exercises:
    - o Market Profile Worksheet
    - o Summary Market Profile

Step 3

Market Research & Analysis

Introduction

There must be a market for your goods or services, or you cannot have a business.

A systematic process of market analysis and research will help you to determine whether there is a market opportunity. Identifying who will buy what you are offering, why they will buy, when they will buy, and how much they are willing to pay are just some of the critical issues touched on in this critical step.

Market research and analysis is a critical activity

Without a market, there are no customers

Without customers, there is no business

This is another step where going to the trouble to gather data and being very honest with yourself is critical to your future success. The good news is that you do not have to be a trained statistician to analyze your market place, nor does the analysis have to be costly.

The rest of the good news is that there are numerous resources where you can find the data and that will help you to understand what the data tells you about your market.

In this Step, you will now determine whether there is in fact a potential market for your business idea. The first section is an article about why market research is so important along with some ideas about how to get started. The worksheet that follows will help you organize your ideas, and show some questions that need to be answered. There are numerous sources of market data – these are shown, along with links to resources in your local area, all to help you answer this critical question:

Is there a market for my business idea?

What are you going to sell?
Who is going to buy it?
Why are they going to buy it from you?

Are there enough customers in your market area that will buy from you, to make the business succeed?

Why Market Research & Analysis?

The market research or study is one of the most critical parts of the whole planning process. It establishes the base for the feasibility analysis and sales forecasting. A market study identifies target customers, the size of the potential demand and the competition, and includes a comparison of the company's products or services with those of the competition. Market research and analysis often seems to be the most difficult of the planning activities, yet that doesn't have to be so. There is a great deal of market information available, even for highly innovative new ideas. Taking the time to find this data and understand it is an essential part of your planning process.

Who is your TARGET?

Market research starts with target marketing. Very simply, target marketing means identifying the "target" of your sales and business activities.

The clearer you can be, the more accurate your analysis can be.

Potential customers can be defined by geographic location, socio-economic or ethnic factors, occupation, age, sex, or any of a thousand other factors. Whatever they are, make sure you identity them. There are some key questions you must answer before you get started. Use the *Market Profile Worksheet* (Exercise 3a) to define your target market.

You can obtain information about the size of your market from your chamber of commerce, local planning commission, trade publications, marketing consultants, other businesspersons, schools and colleges. The local chamber of commerce and planning commission are great places to start, not only because they have excellent data readily available, but also because there is usually someone there who will help you find and understand the information you need. The planning commission will have trend analyses and often even have traffic counts for various areas to help in location assessment. The marketing department at your local college or university is another great source of help. It may be possible to work with a professor to develop a market research project that students will perform for you as a part of their class work – an excellent, no-cost resource.

Other excellent sources of information are the Federal Census and state department of labor. The Federal Census data is broken down by many different consumer and business characteristics – even down to neighborhood areas. Find and review the census tracts that are relevant for your market area.

Find marketing help at
www.BUZGate.org

Another valuable resource is Economic & Labor Market Information (ELMI) reports available from your state Department of Labor.

This information provides both profiles of labor market characteristics, showing earning levels for different employment categories, the size of these categories in your area, and a forecast of how these categories are expected to grow or change over the next ten years. The ELMI system also contains community profiles that show differences between community areas.

There are many other excellent resources, especially on the web. The danger though with web-based research is that the sheer quantity a web search can return can be overwhelming, and it is often difficult to know its validity. One of the very best places to use is the local library – and the help of the librarian.

Think about it:

Just because Market Research sounds complex doesn't mean that you shouldn't do it – Actually, you MUST do it as the success of the venture depends on making sure that there will be enough customers for your business to succeed

By the way – It also doesn't have to be complex either

Use your common sense!

Sources of Market Data

The following sources will help you identify and find data you need to help you evaluate the market opportunity for your own business idea:

Census Data

A useful source for demographic data is the US Census Bureau. Here you will discover detailed data on population demographics as well as business statistics including how many, types, and locations.

Link: Search nationally for data at
http://quickfacts.census.gov/qfd/index.html

Competitive Research Data

One of the best ways to find industry data on size, trends, and competition, is through the annual and quarterly filings required by the US Securities Exchange of all publicly traded companies. This information, known as 10k or 10q, is detailed and voluminous. Read what you want, but be aware that the SEC requires these firms to be as truthful as possible.

Link: SEC Filings and Forms (EDGAR) at
http://www.sec.gov/edgar.shtml

Link: Search by specific company at
http://www.freeedgar.com/Search/BeginSearch.asp

Business Credit Information

To obtain credit information on just about any company anywhere, use the Dun and Bradstreet credit reports and search database. There is a charge for certain data. Link: D & B Information Request Form at
http://www.dnb.com/us/

BUZGate.org

The Knowledge Institute's Business Utility Zone Gateway is a small business resource community listing thousands of free and low cost public programs available to help small businesses to get started and grow.

Market Data may be found under the following listings:

- o Business Marketing
- o Business References
- o Business Research
- o Business Statistics

To access this information, go to: www.BUZGate.org, then click on your state, then click on Free Help. Select the categories you want to explore.

The Marketing Concept

Marketing is more than an activity; it is an attitude, a philosophical approach governing all of the decisions made by and for the business. This attitude is expressed as the Marketing Concept, which suggests that a firm should focus all of its efforts on satisfying its customers at a profit.

Instead of trying to get customers to buy what the firm likes to make, or happens to have on hand, the marketing oriented firm tries to produce or sell what its customers want.

There are three key components in meeting the Marketing Concept criteria:

1. A Customer Orientation,
2. An Integrated Company Effort, and
3. A Goal to Increase Profits Rather Than Increase Sales.

A Customer Orientation requires that the firm focus on what the customers (target market) want and need rather than on what the firm may independently choose to produce or market. While these two perspectives may coincide, in many cases they do not. When they are different, the wants and needs of the target market must take precedence over the firm's preferences.

An Integrated Company Effort requires the organization and coordination of the firm's activities towards satisfying the target market's wants and needs. In fact, the actual shape of the firm's organization is depicted by the parameters (or boundaries) of the market and product/service. If each of the firm's activities is viewed as part of a system designed to satisfy the customers' wants and needs (the ones you have chosen to satisfy), the objectives will be set almost automatically.

By setting Profit Rather Than Sales as the firm's goal, you will avoid the error of mistaking increased sales at any cost for progress. If you analyze your firm's operations and opportunities in terms of their profitability rather than sheer volume, you can count on increasing your net profits in short order.

Target Marketing

The idea is simple enough. Every business has a potential market out there somewhere within that broad, fuzzy, agglomeration of persons and organizations that might conceivably be induced to buy your product, service or merchandise.

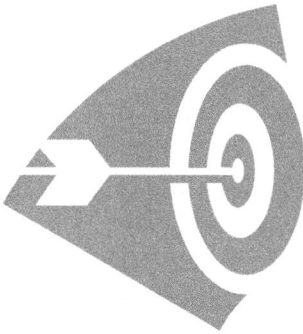

We also know that aiming at the entire broad market would be extremely wasteful; hence the need for Target Marketing. Many possible buyers are, when considered carefully, too far away geographically, can't afford your product, don't want to change suppliers, prefer to shop locally - the list is endless. Recognizing these limitations is a good first step towards identifying your target market.

You must identify, within that broad market of all logically possible buyers, those segments of the population that are most likely to purchase your products.

Why Target Marketing? Think of a target. The bull's eye is small yet, in sporting events, represents the highest points or value when impacted. The first ring just outside of the bull's eye, is a bit larger and easier to hit, but not quite as valuable as the bull's eye. The next ring is larger still, yet represents even less value and so on, as you move outward on the target rings away from the bull's eye. Once off the target, there is no value at all.

Now, suppose that you need $100 in sales to meet your goals. You have a limited number of marketing dollars to invest in attracting these sales - say $15. For the sake of this example, think of each marketing dollar as an arrow. Every bull's eye will net you $10 in sales, the first ring will net $5, the next $3, and the outside ring $1.

It is not difficult to conclude that it will require a few bull's eyes to reach these goals. Therefore, how do you best proceed? While it would not be wise to just blindly fire your arrows randomly, this is exactly what many companies do with their sales/marketing efforts. To maximize your chances of success and minimize your chances of failure, you not only have to take careful aim with each arrow, but also must know the potential return of what you are aiming at.

This example presents the basic concept of Target Marketing. As with competitive archery, you do better taking careful aim than randomly firing all of your arrows. In addition, it is important to look at both those factors that are within your control and those that are outside of your control. For example, how well you aim and shoot is within your control. External factors include how far away is the target, how big is the target, the wind conditions, the light quality, etc. Examples of external factors that will affect the accuracy of your Target Marketing aim include broad economic currents, shifts in style, changes in technologies, new competition, and various political issues. However, by maintaining an awareness of these factors as you prepare your marketing strategies, you can minimize their impact. The point is that both internal and external factors affect a marksman's performance. Marksmanship, as well as return on marketing investment, will improve with practice.

Exercises Step 3: Market Research & Analysis

3a. Market Profile Worksheet

3b. Summary Market Profile

Now on to the exercises....

3a: Market Profile Worksheet

The place to start your Market Research is with what you already know. Write out the answers to the following questions. Don't worry if you don't know or are unsure of the answers. The analysis will show you what you need to know and in the context of why you need to know it. Once you have established what additional information you need and why you need it, the process of finding the information is much easier because it all makes much more sense.

Review each question thoughtfully. Jot down what comes into your mind first. If you don't know the answer, skip that question and move on to the next. Areas left blank will identify issues where further market research and/or the advice of an experienced counselor may help. There are no right or wrong answers. Discuss your answers with your mentor/counselor.

Market Profile Worksheet
1. Who is your market?
2. What is the present size of the market?
3. What percent of the market will you have?
4. What is the markets' growth potential?

Market Profile Worksheet (Continued)
5.   As the market grows, will your share increase or decrease? Why?
6.   Who are your five nearest competitors? a. b. c. d. e.
7.   How is their business: steady, increasing, decreasing, why?
8.   How are their operations similar or dissimilar to yours?
9.   What are their strengths and weaknesses?

A better mousetrap is not sufficient...

- You must tell your customers about it
- There must be...
    - a perceived need
    - a belief that your trap will satisfy the need
    - a willingness to pay a price for it

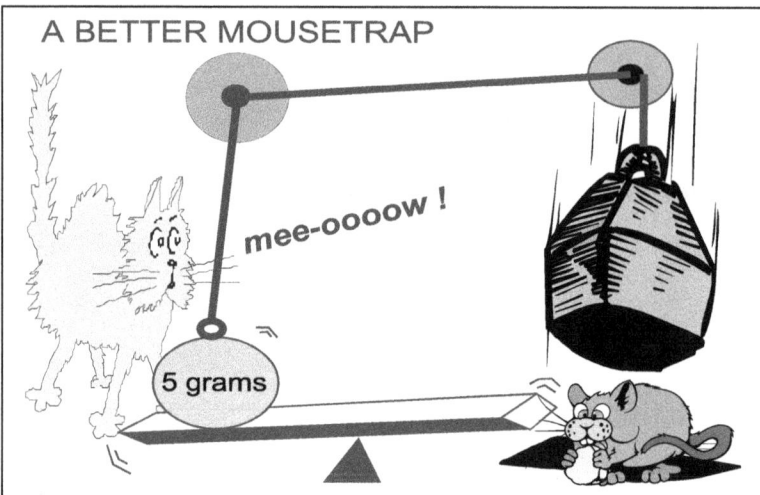

Summary Step 3

In this Step the goal is to examine the reasons you believe that there will be a market for your goods or services. We also showed you a number of sources for market data.

The key to answering this marketing question is to make it all personal.

Marketing Summary
1.   Who will buy your goods/services?
2.   Why will they buy them?
3.   How many are in this group? or groups?
4.   Who is the competition?
5.   Three reasons the potential customers will buy from you

Now on to Step 4...

4

STEP 4

Management Skills

Do I have the skills needed to make this work?

In this Section:

- o Introduction
- o Management Control
- o Strategic Mapping
- o Functional Task Analysis
- o Organizational Mapping Worksheet
- o Exercises:
    - o Management Skills Analysis Worksheet
    - o Management Skills Inventory Worksheet
    - o Summary Management Skills

Step 4

Management Skills

Introduction

Do I have the business skills I need to succeed?

Certain skills and experience are critical to the success of any business. Other skills are essential to the particular business that you may be interested in starting. The way to get started here is to first perform an inventory of the skills and experiences you already have. You can then compare these against the skills and experiences you will need in order to succeed.

What do I know?
&
What don't I know?

The gaps that may exist between what skills you have and what skills you need will show you where you may need to get more training or gain more experience.

If you want to start a restaurant and do not have any experience in the restaurant business, it makes sense to work in a restaurant similar to the one you are interested in and learn what you need to know that way – without risking your own new venture by trial and error learning in your own business.

In this Step, you will now determine whether you have the management skills needed to be successful in your own venture. First we provide an article to read to give you some context and background. This is followed by a worksheet to help you identify your own skills and skill gaps. If you do not have all the skills you require, there are many places where you can receive instruction and help in developing more general business management and technical skills. Determine what training or experience you need, and then find a resource that will meet these needs conveniently and affordably. Resources are listed where you can find needed instruction. Sometimes it is easy to get lost in the jargon. It is no different with these business topics. A glossary of terms is provided at the end of this Workbook to help you to better understand the issues.

- o   Management Control Overview

- o   Management skills inventory – needed business skills

- o   Links of resources to obtain help

Management Control

While success can come to any business as an accidental consequence of floundering around reacting to problems as they emerge, the odds do not favor this happening. There are too many factors that must be organized to reasonably expect that the essential coordination will simply occur.

Good management helps you to make the most efficient use possible out of your scarcest resources: time, people, and money. Planning the productive use of these assets enables you to get the greatest return for your efforts. Control helps make sure that the plans are working as expected and, if not, provides an opportunity to figure out why and bring about the needed change. The key to successful business management is to determine what needs to be done, who will do it, and how you will know when it's done.

Management Questions

- o   What needs to be done?
- o   Who will do it?
- o   How will you know when it's done?

What needs to be done? Functional Task Analysis identifies and describes the different functions or activities that must be performed within the business in order to make sure that all of the operations are performed completely.

The result of this process is a list of the various activities and specific tasks needed for your business to function on a day-to-day basis. It also includes the functions needed for your business to stay tuned to, and respond to change, creatively and proactively.

Large corporations have many top-level officials who are each assigned responsibility for different job functions within the organization. An organizational chart will show these various functional responsibilities through titles such as vice presidents of marketing, production, finance, personnel, planning, and others. Smaller businesses must look at their own operations in a similar way.

Someone must perform the same functions as in the larger organization, or the smaller business cannot operate effectively. It is essential to identify each of these critical areas.

For starters, create your own organizational chart to show all of the same functions represented in a large company, then note beside each how much time it should take on a regular basis.

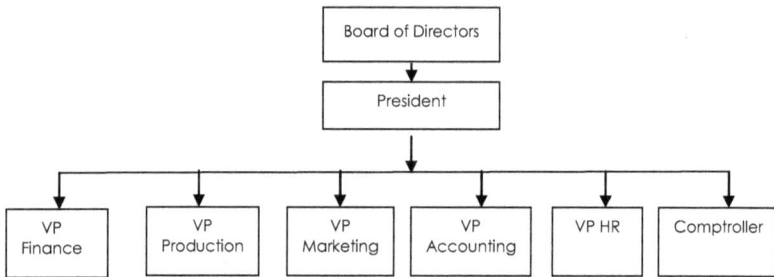

```
                    ┌──────────────────┐
                    │ Board of Directors│
                    └──────────────────┘
                             │
                             ▼
                    ┌──────────────────┐
                    │    President     │
                    └──────────────────┘
                             │
    ┌──────┬──────┬──────────┼──────────┬──────┬──────────┐
    ▼      ▼      ▼          ▼          ▼      ▼
┌───────┐┌───────┐┌───────┐┌────────┐┌──────┐┌──────────┐
│  VP   ││  VP   ││  VP   ││  VP    ││VP HR ││Comptroller│
│Finance││Production││Marketing││Accounting││      ││          │
└───────┘└───────┘└───────┘└────────┘└──────┘└──────────┘
```

Once the key functional areas are identified, define the related tasks that must be performed to support each activity. One way to efficiently approach this is to make a list of the work tasks needed in the company. This list can be generated from job descriptions and/or from an actual analysis of the workflow process such as through a daily task log analysis. It is far better to use a systematic approach here than an informal one. Relying on your memory will guarantee that you will omit some important activities.

. Any business can be looked at as a system composed of interdependent and interrelated parts. Each component part must be recognized as an important area of responsibility and treated accordingly. This will help to assure that some functional areas do not fall through the cracks. At the same time, these parts must all function together in harmony if the system is to operate effectively. This latter side of the issue is a concept known as functional unity. It helps to keep the different parts of the system in perspective or balance even when each segment sends signals and makes demands as though it is the most important. All of these concepts simply reinforce the need for balance and control.

Who will do it? Once you have completed the Functional Task Analysis, it is a matter of associating people with the activities. Careful work in the first part of this exercise will produce a very specific list of tasks that must be performed, along with an estimate of how much time is required to maintain each activity on a regular basis. The next step is to attach the name of some individual to every single one of these tasks. Here it is critical to make sure that you have the right people for the tasks that need to be done; that they thoroughly understand what needs to be done; and are motivated to do it. In most smaller companies, the human resources will make or break the company!

Once the appropriate employees are associated with each element of work from the Functional Task Analysis, the work structure is laid out in a formal manner through a process of Organizational Mapping. The result here is a highly detailed version of the organizational chart, complete with tasks, sub-tasks, time requirements, and individual names.

How will you know if, when, and how well the work is done?

As you set up the task assignments, identify the ways that you will clearly be able to determine whether or not they are being accomplished.

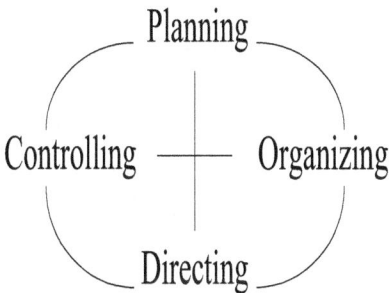

Planning

Controlling —— Organizing

Directing

This is important not only in the general sense of running your business and making sure that things are staying on track, but is critical in delegating responsibilities to your subordinates. At the end of a given project, you and your subordinates must be able to clearly agree about what was or was not accomplished during a given period of time.

The work plan process is the route by which these activities are assigned. The establishment of evaluation criteria is the predetermination of how effectiveness in the various areas will be measured. The more specific these criteria can be, and effectively communicated to each employee, the more accurate will be the behavior within the organization. The information required to monitor these activities can flow to you as a series of deviation reports where the actual results are compared with the projected results.

Work can then be assigned to specific individuals. First, cover each task with a specific personnel assignment, then total up the time assignments for each individual. You will cover all of the tasks and be able to quickly spot areas where any individual may have been over (or under) committed. Following these activities, a Time Planning Schedule allows you to assign the work to each key employee on a weekly basis and agree with him or her on the feasibility and priority of the various tasks. Through a brief mutual review at the end of the week, you can quickly evaluate what was actually done and plan for the upcoming week. This is a powerful communication as well as management control and monitoring tool.

Organizational Mapping allows you to effectively and efficiently define the tasks within your company, estimate the relative percentage of staff time required by each, and then assign the tasks so defined to specific individuals within the organization. This process will also show where new individuals must be recruited to fill certain job requirements. Don't forget to schedule yourself, but be fair. None of us has infinite time. Even if we choose to work 18 hours per day, after a while we loose our efficiency and so our edge. Be sensible.

Organizational Mapping is always a very interesting and valuable exercise. An example worksheet follows on the next page.

Organizational Mapping Worksheet

Instructions: In Part I, list each task with a specific personnel assignment. In Part II, list personnel with all task assigned in Part I. You will quickly be able to spot areas where key individuals have been over (or under) committed.

I. Functional Task Analysis			
Task #	List all tasks needing to be performed	Hours/Week Required	Personnel Assigned

II. Staff Commitment					
List all personnel assigned above	Task #	Hours used per task	Total hours used per person/week	Total hours available per person/week	Balance of hours positive / negative

Exercises Step 4: Management Skills

4a. Management Skills Analysis

4b. Management Skills Inventory

4c. Summary Step 4

Now on to the exercises….

4a. Management Skills Analysis

Identifying needed business skills – Taking an inventory of where your business management strengths and weaknesses are is a very useful planning exercise. Not being strong in certain areas of business management is only a problem if you don't recognize it. By recognizing it, you may choose to secure additional training or the services of someone who is proficient in the areas where you lack skills.

The following worksheet will help you take an inventory of your management strengths and weaknesses. In answering each question, consider tasks that you've performed in prior positions, volunteer work, community services, personal characteristics and other traits that define how you tend to manage situations and resources.

Read each question carefully and respond as honestly and as creatively as possible. Your answers will help identify where your strengths are and where you may want to secure the services of others, pursue additional training, and/or gain direct experience. Think about your answers and talk them over with someone else – your partner, mentor or counselor. Using this as a basis for discussion can often uncover other issues affecting the business development process.

List areas where you have had a management role in the past
Work Positions Held (Position/Responsibilities)
Volunteer Work (Position/Responsibilities)
Community Service (Position/Responsibilities)
Other Projects (Position/Responsibilities)

4b. Management Skills Inventory

Instructions: Check the box that best matches your self-perceived skill level per each category

Evaluate your skills in the areas below			
Business Management Discipline	**Perceived Strengths**		
Working With People	**High**	**Medium**	**Low**
Communication, verbal and written			
Negotiating Skills			
Resolving conflict			
Coordinating human resources			
Accepting responsibility			
Social Skills			
Professional conduct			
Organization and Planning	**High**	**Medium**	**Low**
Establishing goals			
Achieving goals			
Managing time			
Maintaining work schedules			
Cash Management	**High**	**Medium**	**Low**
Establishing budgets			
Negotiating deals			
Bill paying			
Loan/credit history			
Fundraising			
Record keeping			
Tax Preparation			
Maintaining profits			
Selling Ideas, Products and Services	**High**	**Medium**	**Low**
Ability to convince others / Presentation skills			
Meeting sales goals			
Overcoming objections			
Facilitating Outcomes			
Managing Resources	**High**	**Medium**	**Low**
Effectively delegating			
Monitoring progress			
Motivating others			
Dealing with change			
Overcoming challenges			
Resourcefulness			
Total Checks in Each Column			

Evaluate your skills in the areas below (Continued)			
Business Management Discipline	**Perceived Strengths**		
Risk Taking	High	Medium	Low
Self confidence			
Strategic planning			
Assess outcomes			
Follow through			
Reward oriented			
Independence and Leadership	High	Medium	Low
Leadership skills			
Self disciplined			
Self directed			
Work independently			
Consistency			
Personality Traits	High	Medium	Low
Over achiever			
Take charge			
Work hard			
Patient			
Determined			
Performance Standards			
Product, Service or other Specialized Knowledge	High	Medium	Low
Research			
Information processing			
Knowledge integration			
Customer Service	High	Medium	Low
Problem solving			
Delivering on promises			
Satisfying needs			
Scoring			
Total Checks per Column			
Total Checks from Prior Page			
Total Check per Column			
Multiply total in each column by the factor shown	X 5	X 3	X 1
Enter values for each column			
Total three columns for your total score			

Evaluation:

If you scored between 260 and 208, you have an excellent aptitude and experience to be a manager of your own venture.

If you scored between 207 and 156, you have reasonable aptitude and experience to be a manager of your own venture.

If you scored below 155, you should seriously reevaluate your readiness to launch your own venture.

Look at the areas where you were low, and determine what you can do to improve your own skills – take some management courses, or find some one to work with you who can compliment your lower skill areas.

Four Key Management Activities

o   Planning: Setting goals and objectives for the organization, developing work maps showing how these goals and objectives are to be accomplished

o   Organizing: Bringing together resources, people, capital and equipment, determining the most effective way of accomplishing goals, integrating resources

o   Directing: Ensuring that the required work functions are performed, identifying who will do given tasks in and making sure that they are done. Motivating is the other approach here – Directing means making people do things; Motivating means making them want to do these things, then letting them do them

o   Controlling: Feedback of results; follow up to compare accomplishments with plans and to make appropriate adjustments where outcomes have deviated from expectations

Summary Step 4

In this Step the goal is to examine your own management skills and experiences as a way of determining your own readiness for starting and operating your own venture.

The worksheets provided a means for you to evaluate whether you have the skills needed to be successful in your own venture, along with a way to inspect the management needs of each part of your venture.

The key to answering this management question is to make it all personal.

Management Skills Summary
1.   What are your greatest strengths?
2.   What are your greatest weaknesses?
3.   What will you do to complement your areas of weakness?

Now on to Step 5....

5

STEP 5

Business Plan

Do I have a complete business plan?

In this Section:

- o   Introduction
- o   Planning Overview
- o   Guidelines for Writing a Business Plan
- o   Planning Outline
- o   Sample Business Plans
- o   Exercises:
    - o   Business Definition Worksheet
    - o   Summary Business Planning

Step 5

Business Plan

Introduction

Do I have a complete business plan?

The business plan is the place where you organize and present all of the ideas about what the business is, how it works, and what resources are needed to make it all work. It is important that you do the actual work of developing the plan. There are many resources that can help you develop the plan, but it will be your business and so it must be your ideas and your plan.

> The Business Plan is your strategy for profitably operating your business

A planning overview is presented here first. Effective planning requires a certain attitude or mind-set. This will help you understand the planning issues.

A business plan outline is presented to help you organize your ideas and answer questions about how the business will function. This is followed by a planning worksheet to help you start to capture key elements for your own plan. You will see that you have already started the process in the earlier Steps.

Many times, people are afraid of writing their own plan. They feel that it is a complicated process and that they do not have the writing ability to put their ideas on paper effectively. The process is actually quite simple.

Start by addressing the issues in each section of the planning outline. The answers will provide the meat and potatoes of the actual plan itself. Links to sample plans are provided. Sometimes seeing how someone else tackled the issues helps to better understand the process.

An effective business plan is actually a model of how the business operates

A good business plan shows how the business will actually operate, and should provide valuable guidance once the new business is started.

The next Step on forecasting will show you how to develop the forecasts and budgets that support your plan.

Once you have developed the framework for your own business idea, you may want to seek some assistance in actually writing the plan – there are many excellent resources to help you with this process.

- o Guidelines for Writing a Business Plan
- o Business Plan Outline
- o Business Definition Worksheet
- o Sample Business Plans
- o Business Planning Resources

Key to Effective Business Planning

Effective Business Planning Starts With Goals

Are the goals tangible?
- Can results be measured? Counted? Tracked?

Do these goals make sense?
- Is % Market Penetration > Total Market?
- Is Business Growth > Business Capacity?

Have you planned realistically?
- Do you have enough manpower, room, supervision, money, desire?

Guidelines for Writing a Business Plan

Why should you go to the trouble of creating a written business plan? There are at least three major reasons:

- o The process of constructing a business plan, including the thought you put in before beginning to write it, forces you to take an objective look at your business project in its entirety.

- o The finished product, your business plan, is an operating tool which, properly used, will help you manage your business and work toward its success.

- o The completed business plan communicates your ideas to others and provides the basis for your financing proposal.

By taking a critical look at your business, you can identify areas of weakness and strength, pinpoint needs you might otherwise overlook, spot problems before they arise, and begin planning how you can best achieve your business goals.

Purposes of Planning

- o Feasibility Analysis
- o Goal Setting
- o Developmental Framework
- o Operational Guide
- o Communication Tool

Your business plan helps you to establish reasonable objectives and determine how to best accomplish them. It also helps to highlight problems as they arise and aids you in identifying their sources, thus suggesting ways to solve them. It may even help you to avoid some problems altogether.

Finally, your business plan provides the information that will be needed by others to evaluate your venture, especially if you need to seek outside financing. A thorough business plan automatically becomes a complete financing proposal, which will meet the requirements of most financiers.

Business planning establishes the framework for business success. It enables the development of a logical and coherent plan of action for any business. It does require knowing what to do and how to do it. It does require developing a program and following it. However, all of this can be quite straightforward. The objective here is to show you what needs to be done and how to do it.

Effective business planning entails time and effort. However, in order for your plan to work, it is important that you do as much of this work as possible. If you are already in business, taking time to plan may seem impossible. Nevertheless, while you can hire people to do the work in your business, you cannot hire someone to do the planning. Others can assist you in the process, but the plan is for your venture and so must be based on your ideas and assumptions. A professionally prepared business plan won't do you any good if you don't understand it thoroughly. This essential understanding comes from being involved with its development from the outset. A through business plan will help you avoid mistakes saving you effort, time, and money.

Remember...
Planning without action
is a waste of time

No business plan, no matter how carefully constructed and no matter how thoroughly understood, will be of any value unless you use it.

If you are not in business but are trying to determine whether or not your business idea makes sense, or if you are getting started, the planning process outlined here is your most important task.

Going into business is difficult at best. Over half of all new businesses fail within the first two years of operation; over 90 percent fail within the first ten years. A major reason for these failures is lack of planning. The best way to enhance your chances of success is to plan and follow through on your planning. Don't feel that the plan was written for your financing sources; this may well be an important function, but it is secondary to the action implications. Above all, don't put it in the bottom drawer of your desk and forget it.

Your business plan can help you avoid going into a business venture that is doomed to failure. If your proposed venture is marginal at best, the business plan will show you why and may help you avoid the high tuition of business failure. It is far cheaper not to begin an ill-fated business than to learn by experience what your business plan could have taught you at a cost of several hours of concentrated work.

Define Your Strategic Objectives

The first step of any planning process is to define the outcome objectives. What is the "end goal" of the planning process, the strategic purpose? The 'strategic purpose' is a broad picture of the company, and is comprised of strategic objectives, or goals. To be useful, these goals must be clearly stated, specific, and objective. Generally for smaller organizations, the time frame is three years. This time horizon can be longer, but three years is about the maximum time span that can be planned within with any confidence that the anticipated results are likely to happen. Detailed action planning for periods longer than this becomes very difficult as the factors affecting the business outcomes are too vague and unpredictable.

Time Lining

The three-year goals are the broad destination targets. Once defined, we can begin to determine what needs to be done to get there. The longer-term goals are broken into sub-targets, typically expressed as goals for year 2, and year 1. The 1-2 year targets help you to define what needs to be done in the near term to lay the groundwork for the longer-term goals.

Time Lining

How can we establish a logical sequence of events from today to a future goal?

The Answer:

Start with a three year goal

| | 3rd Year $$, ## |

Add the two year intermediate goal

| 2rd Year $$, ## | 3rd Year $$, ## |

Add the one year intermediate goal

| 1st Year $$, ## | 2rd Year $$, ## | 3rd Year $$, ## |

Then break the one year goal into 12 months

| 1 | 2 | 3 | 4 | 5 | 6 | 7 | 8 | 9 | 10 | 11 | 12 | 1st Year $$, ## |

Now it is possible to identify activities needed next month, next week and even tomorrow to achieve the longer term goals

Business Planning Process

The information and ideas collected during the business planning process take a particular form when organized into a formal business plan. The material should be organized in a rational order so that it leads the reader from point to point and then to a logical conclusion. The sequence is important because each idea and each section builds on the one before.

A planning mindset

Visualize the business operation and activities; then describe what is happening

The planning outline suggested below is the result of reviewing and evaluating thousands of plans. Consequently, this format is designed to satisfy the requirements of most lenders, especially commercial bankers and the U.S. Small Business Administration.

More complex ventures, particularly those seeking venture capital and other more specialized forms of financing, will require more highly detailed plans.

Certain material in the business plan is designed to set the stage. This material, often called the *Front Matter*, includes the *Cover Sheet*, *Statement of Purpose*, and *Table of Contents*. The *Statement of Purpose* is especially important as an introduction to the plan because it informs the reader what to expect. Following the *Front Matter*, the plan is divided into two major sections; *Description of the Business* and *Financial Data*. These sections are followed by appropriate supporting documents. The *Description of the Business* is the written explanation of what the business is, how it works, and why it will succeed. The *Financial Data* is the quantification of the written portion. It is the numerical display of the nature and effect of the assumptions made in the first section and the demonstration of viability for the overall operational strategy. Developing the *Financial Data* section is the topic of the next Session on Forecasting.

The planning process, no matter how carefully followed, does not guarantee your way to success, but it will substantially reduce your chances of failure. Though this planning effort may be hard work, the dividends will far outweigh the costs.

Plan what needs to happen - then do it – Common Sense!

Business Plan Outline

COVER SHEET - Name of business, names of principals, address and phone number of the business.

STATEMENT OF PURPOSE

TABLE OF CONTENTS

I. THE BUSINESS
    a.   Description of the Business
    b.   Market
    c.   Competition
    d.   Operations
    e.   Location(s)
    f.   Management
    g.   Personnel
    h.   Application and Expected Effect of Loan/Investment
    i.   Development Schedule
    j.   Summary

II. FINANCIAL DATA
    a.   Sources and Applications of Funding
    b.   Capital Equipment List
    c.   Balance Sheet
    d.   Breakeven Analysis
    e.   Income Projections (Profit and Loss Statements)
        i.   Three-year Summary
        ii.   Detail by Month (First Year)
        iii.   Detail by Quarter (Second and Third Years)
        iv.   Notes of Explanation
    f.   Pro-Forma Cash Flow
        i.   Three-year Summary
        ii.   Detail by Month (First Year)
        iii.   Detail by Quarter (Second and Third Years)
        iv.   Notes of Explanation
    g.   Historical Financial Reports for Existing Business
        i.   Balance Sheets for Past Three Years
        ii.   Income Statements for Past Three Years
        iii.   Tax Returns

III. SUPPORTING DOCUMENTS
Personal resumes, job descriptions, personal financial statements, credit reports, letters of reference, letters of intent, copies of leases, contracts, legal documents, and anything else relevant to the plan.

Strategic Mapping

Strategic Mapping represents a rational approach to business development

- o It provides an understandable way to deal with complexity – without getting lost in the confusion

- o We build the business strategy piece by piece, yet we always know that the parts add up to the whole

- o The modular business development process represents a modular control system

Planning and Control = Business Success

Exercises Step 5: Business Plan

5a. Business Definition

5b. Summary Step 5

Now on to the exercises….

5a: Business Definition

Throughout this workbook, you already have been, and will continue to be, developing all of the components of a sound business plan. Below are questions that relate to particular aspects of defining the business.

Review each question thoughtfully. Jot down what comes into your mind first. If you don't know how to answer, skip that question and move on to the next. Areas left blank will identify issues where further thought and the advice of experienced counselors or consultants may help. There are no right or wrong answers. Think about your answers and talk them over with someone else – your partner, mentor or counselor. Using this as a basis for discussion can often uncover other issues affecting the business development process.

Defining the Business
Describe what your business will do and/or what need(s) it will satisfy
Describe your target market – who your business will serve
Describe the competition and how you will gain market share

Defining the Business (Continued)

Describe the operation – Hours, suppliers, other relevant aspects

Describe where the business will be located and why

Describe who will be part of the management team and why – what skills do they bring?

List other personnel that will be needed – are they available? And at what price?

Sample Business Plans

Sometimes the best learning tool is to look at what others have done.

The US Small Business Administration (SBA) co-endorsed website listed below provides links to 60 sample business plans. Follow the link to visit this site and choose a sample plan or plans to review. However, keep in mind that this exercise provides reference points for you to develop your own plan. It is your own business and so should be your own plan.

Instructions:

- o Visit the link: http://www.bplans.com/samples/sba.cfm
- o Scan the alphabetical list of business plan types
- o Click on the business plan(s) you want to review
- o Review the business plan outline and make notes regarding content that you view helpful to your own planning efforts

Business Plan Counseling

There are many free public agency programs and resources available to help you develop a business plan and with many other aspects of starting and managing a business. Throughout this workbook, we have directed you to the Business Utility Zone Gateway, listing thousands of free and low cost public programs available to help small businesses to get started and grow. These public assistance agencies exist to help you with various aspects of your business objectives and do so at no or little charge. You will find an alphabetical listing organized by town of the organizations and people that are available to help you develop an appropriate action strategy.

To access this information, use this link: www.BUZGate.org, then click on your state, then click on Free Help. Select the Business Counseling category.

Summary Step 5

In this Step the goal is to begin to develop a description of the business you want to create. In the Defining the Business worksheet, you began to set down some of your ideas about your new venture. We also provided links to sample business plans and other sources of help in the process.

Now, summarize you business idea and discuss the ideas with someone else – your partner, mentor or counselor. Using this as a basis for discussion can often uncover other issues affecting the business development process. But remember – this is you plan for your idea – the key to developing a successful business plan and strategy is to make it all personal

Business Definition Summary
1.   What is your business?
2.   Why will it succeed?

Business Planning Assistance

We direct your attention to www.BUZGate.org a number of times throughout this Workbook because BUZGate is such a rich resource database and network. It is also free to any user. Use BUZGate to connect with local, regional and national government and nonprofit agency programs that offer no- and low-cost business planning assistance.

www.BUZGate.org

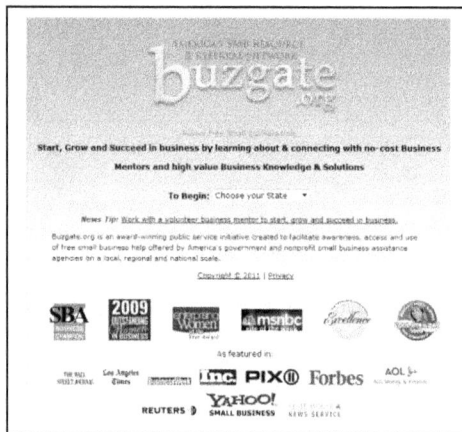

Choose a state to learn about programs such as:

- Small Business Development Centers (SBDC)
- Women's Business Centers (WBC)
- SCORE Counselor's to America's Small Business (SCORE)
- U.S. Small Business Administration Office of Veterans Business Development (OVBD)
- MicroMentor

6

STEP 6

Forecasting

Do I have a realistic forecast of revenues and costs?

In this Section:

- o Introduction
- o Why Forecast?
- o Forecasting – 7 Steps
- o Breakeven Analysis
- o Cash Flow Management
- o Financial Calculators
- o Exercises:
    - o Revenue / Expense Worksheet
    - o Expense Worksheet
    - o Calculate Your Breakeven
    - o Financial Calculators
    - o Profit / Loss Worksheet
    - o Strategic Mapping Worksheet
    - o Summary Step 6

Step 6

Forecasting

Introduction

Why forecast?

Forecasting is where you will determine and organize the financial information for your business, showing costs and revenues. The forecasts become your budget. There is nothing mysterious about forecasting – it is a thoughtful process of thinking about each part of the business operation and determining what kinds of expenses will be generated by these activities. Think about your rent, phone system and all other operational issues that have associated costs. The process will help you to also identify the sources and amounts of revenues that will be generated.

The Forecasting Model	
Revenue	How Much / What Source(s)
Expenses	How Much / What Source(s)
Profit (Loss)	Revenue minus Expense

Forecasting may seem like a complex and mysterious process – you are in fact guessing about what may happen in the future. While you are guessing about what may happen in the future, it is possible to do so in a very careful framework that helps you to make those guesses as accurate as possible – and so as valuable as possible. We have included a fair amount of information in this section – take and use what makes sense to you. Just keep in mind that the equation remains very simple:

o How much revenue are you going to expect? Why?

o How much in costs are you going to expect? Why?

o Are there more revenues than costs? If not, why?

Read the next section, "Why Forecast," to get an idea of what you are doing and why. The section following that article, "Forecasting – the Seven Steps," will help you think through this process, and give you a format to list your sources of expenses and revenues. Two separate sections, one on Cash Flow and one on Breakeven Analysis will help you further in understanding the forecasting process. A financial calculator is also provided to help in calculating ratios and looking at other relationships of the financial data.

Once the data is assembled, if you need help organizing this data into an actual forecast, you can sit down with a resource professional. The good news is that you will have already done the hard part. You have thought through how the business functions, what costs are associated, and how you are going to generate revenues. Once you have this information, they can then show you how the data is used in developing a forecast of your operation for the next two or three years.

o Why Forecast?

o Forecasting – 7 Steps

o Cash Flow Article

o Breakeven Article

o Financial Calculators

o Resources for help

Why Forecast?

Forecasting or projections are the core of the financial data in any business plan. Forecasting is a process of projecting what will happen in the future. In order to get anywhere, you need to identify your destination before you can determine the best route for getting there. The same is true in your business. Forecasting is a process of identifying that destination and then establishing a rough map for your businesses' future activities. It's not 100% accurate, but accurate enough to locate prominent hazards and to establish direction for the business to follow.

What are your revenues?
What are your costs?
Do revenues exceed costs?
If not, why not?

Forecasting is based on carefully reasoned assumptions, quantified in a systematic way to make your projections about what will happen in the future as accurate as possible. By taking a systematic approach to forecasting, you gain deeper knowledge and understanding of your business.

Add the concept of break-even analysis (This is explained in the Breakeven article), and you have a powerful tool to improve decisions regarding expansion, pricing, product mix, advertising, staffing, and many other areas of your business management system.

The final product of your forecasting effort becomes your projected cash flow (This is explained in the Cash Flow article), the basis of the cash budget, which in turn is the primary tool for controlling your business. The purpose of the forecasting process is twofold: it affords an excellent opportunity to review the past and it provides the best guide to the future your business can have.

Forecasting often seems like a very mysterious process. Obviously, no one can know for sure what is going to happen in the future. It is possible, though, to make reasonably accurate predictions based on a logical assessment of the facts that are available to you now. There is no magic to it, no crystal ball. There is instead, a careful analysis of past and current business practices, a degree of extrapolation of current trends (sales, expenses, major economic shifts such as inflation, and others), and a great deal of creative examination, evaluation, and revision of the assumptions you use to operate your business.

Forecasting – Looking to the Future

Revenues over time
Variable Costs over time
Gross Profits over time
Fixed Costs over time
Net Profits over time

Exercises Step 6: Forecasting

6a. Revenue / Expense Worksheet

6b. Expense Worksheet

6c. Calculate Your Breakeven

6d. Financial Calculators

6e. Profit / Loss Worksheet

6f: Strategic Mapping Worksheet

6g. Summary Step 6

As you proceed through this Step, you will find articles interspersed with the exercises. Read the articles carefully and think about how they relate to you and your business.

Now on to the exercises.....

6a: Revenue/Expense Worksheet

Developing a forecast often seems like a mysterious process, but it is no more complex than listing the revenues you expect to receive through your sales activities and the expenses you will incur in securing those sales and operating the business.

List the various sources of revenue you expect to earn, and the expense categories you are likely to incur. This exercise is just to get you thinking about these issues – there is no right or wrong. This is a place to start with your rough thinking. These items will become part of your Forecasting Worksheet and are further refined later in this step.

Once again, discuss these ideas with your mentor or counselor to gain perspective and improve your ideas.

6a: Revenue/Expense Worksheet

Revenue / Expense Worksheet	
Sources of Revenue	**Annual Sales Amount**
1.	
2.	
3.	
4.	
5.	
Expense Categories	**Anticipated Annual Costs**
1.	
2.	
3.	
4.	
5.	
6.	
7	
8.	
9.	
10.	
11.	
12.	
13	
14.	
15.	

Forecasting – The Seven Steps

Effective forecasting can be achieved by following a seven-step process. It involves a systematic analysis of the current and projected structure of the business, a break-even analysis, and various ways of determining reasonable growth patterns for your operation.

1. Identify all FIXED and VARIABLE costs

    Any business will generate expenses over the course of a year. These expenses are either "fixed" or "variable." Fixed costs do not change with changes in the level of sales or operations; variable costs change relative to changes in sales or operations.

    List all expenses (costs); then separate into Fixed and Variable

    Make a list of all expenses you think you will encounter. For most businesses, a great deal of helpful information is available.

    If you are involved in a start-up or expansion, or even if you are in a stable, ongoing business situation and are trying to make your operation more efficient, there are various sources of help. Your accountant, because he is familiar with the cost structures of a variety of different businesses, will be able to help you make sure that you have identified all of the expense categories you can reasonably expect. In addition, various publications such as the Annual Statement Studies (Robert Morris Associates) show average operating expenses for a wide range of small businesses across the country. Trade associations and industry publications are still another source of such information.

2. Determine your BREAKEVEN sales level

    Breakeven is where the business does not have a profit or a loss.

    Breakeven
    Total Revenue = Total Costs
    There is no profit and no loss

    Breakeven is the level of sales necessary to cover all of the fixed and variable costs. Here is the short version – see the Breakeven article following for more detail.

Breakeven is when all of your costs are covered – no profit, no loss. The problem in determining this point is with the fixed costs. If there were no fixed costs, and as long as you were making a profit on each item you sell, there would be no breakeven issue.

Assuming that you have fixed costs (such as rent, electricity, Internet, etc) of $1,000 per month, and you sell your products for $10 and make $4 on each unit, how many units do you have to sell? The answer is in the $4 that you make on each unit – this is called the gross profit. If this number is shown as a percentage of sales (sales/gross profit), it is called the gross margin. Here it would be $10/$4 = 40%. So, how many times do you have to repeat the sale that produces the $4 in profit to cover your fixed costs? Simple – divide the fixed costs by the $4.

Using this information, we can quickly determine how many units are needed. Divide the fixed costs of $1,000 by the gross profit of $4, and you have your breakeven point.

$$\$1,000/\$4 = 250 \text{ units}$$

Let's check the math:

250 units times $10 per unit equals $2,500 in Total Sales. The cost of manufacturing the units needed for this level of sales is 250 times the sales price minus the Gross Profit ($10 - $4 = $6) or 250 units times $6 cost per unit equals $1,500 in costs (also called Cost of Goods Sold). If we subtract the total cost of $1,500 from the total sales of $2,500, we have a Gross Profit of $1,000 which exactly equals the Fixed Costs of $1,000. The business has neither a profit nor a loss. This is your breakeven.

Total Sales (250 units x $10/unit)	$2,500
Cost of Goods Sold (250 units x $6 per unit)	$1,500
Gross Profit	$1,000
Fixed Costs	$1,000
Net Profit / Loss	-0-

We can do the same thing (even quicker) when we know the Gross Margin. Here we already calculated the Gross Margin as 40%. If we simply divide the Fixed Cost of $1,000 by 40% as a decimal (.40), we get the same answer:

Fixed Costs ($1,000) divided by Gross Margin (.40) equals $2,500

3. Evaluate the ODDS of reaching breakeven

Once you know the level of sales you must reach before making a profit, how reasonable is this target? What are the odds of reaching this breakeven sales level? Convert the sales level into operational measures.

Breakeven equals how many bowls of soup?

If you are a restaurant selling soup, how many bowls of soup must you sell to reach breakeven? How does this measure relative to your capacity to cook and serve soup? How does it relate to your market?

If you can't say that your concept or operation makes sense at this point (as an expansion needing 110% of the market, for example), then reexamine your plans. The process of reexamination may make you aware of new solutions. In any case, recognizing limitations through this type of analysis is much cheaper than charging blindly into a disaster. If it isn't going to work at all, acknowledge it at this point and save yourself the agony of failure.

4. Determine WHEN you will reach breakeven

Virtually all new businesses will start out at a loss, simply because it takes awhile to get started, for new customers to find out where your business is, and to learn that you are providing goods and services which will satisfy their wants and needs. It is essential to predict as accurately as possible how long it will take for your start-up operation to reach its breakeven point because the sum of the monthly operating deficits up to that point will help you to determine how much working capital you will require for your business.

How fast will you
add new customers?

For an ongoing business, past sales experience is a good guide.

Another way to achieve the needed result is by calculating how many new customers you can add per month, how many old customers you can retain, frequency of repeat sales, and the average dollar sale per customer.

5. Calculate your CONTINGENCY RESERVE

A contingency reserve is your backup working capital. Most businesses lose money when they start-up. Expansions usually behave similarly. By definition, these situations will lose money until they reach their breakeven level of sales. The amount of this loss can be calculated through your cash flow analysis and is the amount that you must have available to invest in the business as working capital.

If it takes longer to reach the breakeven level than you first anticipated, the loss will continue and you will have to invest more capital. It is only common sense to have this additional working capital available as a cash or contingency reserve. The contingency reserve can be calculated by projecting two levels of growth: reasonable growth and pessimistic growth.

The amount you should plan for is the negative cash flow difference between the two projections. Clearly, if you thought that there was a reasonable possibility of not having any sales, you should reconsider the project!

6. Develop your INCOME FORECAST

The parts of the process for income forecasting have now been assembled. In STEP 1, you identified your FIXED and VARIABLE expenses. In STEPS 2 through 5, you experimented with different ways of constructing SALES FORECASTS. Using these understandings, now you can continue these steps so that you can inspect the changes that you expect in your business month by month. This will show you the actual profit or loss that you can expect from your venture, and becomes your projected or pro forma income statement.

7. Translate the income forecasts into a CASH FLOW

    The PROJECTED CASH FLOW is the basis of your cash budget. It shows the TIMING of cash flows and enables you to ensure that you will have adequate cash reserves as well as working capital.

    Cash Inflow must equal or exceed cash outflow or the business cannot survive

    For a new venture, or for a rapidly growing venture, it is likely that cash will flow out more rapidly than it comes in.

    The difference between the cash inflows and the cash outflows must come from somewhere.

    Cash flow forecasting enables you to predict both the size and timing of this kind of temporary operating deficit. By adding to this figure a cushion for unexpected emergencies (Step 5), you can figure how much cash reserve you will need to remain solvent. See the Cash Flow article.

SUMMARY

FORECASTING is based on carefully reasoned assumptions, quantified in a systemic way to make your projections about what will happen in the future as accurate as possible. By taking a systematic approach to forecasting, you gain a deeper knowledge and understanding of your business. The final product of your forecasting effort becomes your projected cash flow, the basis of the cash budget, which in turn is a primary tool for controlling your business.

Good business planning is a primary key to business success.

6b: Expense Worksheet

Now that you have considered your costs through *Forecasting- The 7 Steps*, consider your costs and divide them into the Fixed and Variable categories. Use the following worksheet.

Instructions: List the various expense categories you think are likely to incur, and separate them into the Fixed and Variable categories. This exercise is just to get you thinking about these issues – there is no right or wrong answer. This is a place to start with your rough thinking. These items will become part of your Forecasting Worksheet and are further refined later in this session. Once again, discuss these ideas with your mentor or counselor to gain perspective and improve your ideas.

Expense Worksheet	
Variable Expense Categories	**Anticipated Cost per Unit**
1. Materials	
2. Supplies	
3. Production Labor	
4.	
5.	
Fixed Expense Categories	**Anticipated Monthly Costs**
1. Rent	
2. Telephone	
3. Electric	
4. Insurance	
5.	
6.	
7	
8.	
9.	
10.	
11.	
12.	
13	
14.	
15.	

Breakeven Analysis

Breakeven analysis is a powerful management tool, and one that is critical in planning, decision-making, and expense control. Breakeven analysis can be invaluable in determining whether to buy or lease, expand into a new area, build a new plant, and many other such considerations. Breakeven analysis can also show the impact on your business of changing your price structure – As the price goes down (and so your gross margin goes down), breakeven shoots up - usually very rapidly. Breakeven analysis will not force a decision, of course, but it will provide you with additional insights into the effects of important business decisions on your bottom line.

Breakeven refers to the level of sales necessary to cover all of the fixed and variable costs.

> **Fixed Costs** are those costs or expenses that are expected to remain fairly constant over a reasonable period of time. These costs are relatively unaffected by changes in output or sales up to the point where the level of operation reaches the capacity of the existing facilities. At that point, major changes would have to be made, such as the expansion of existing plant and equipment or the construction of new facilities. Such actions would increase the fixed costs. However, under normal operating conditions, the fixed costs (also referred to as indirect costs, overhead, or burden) will remain constant. Some examples of fixed costs include rent or mortgage payments, interest on loans, executive and office salaries, and general office expenses.

> **Variable Costs** are those costs or expenses that vary or change directly with output. These costs are associated with production and/or selling and are frequently identified as "costs of goods sold." As compared with the fixed costs, which continue whether the firm is doing business or not, variable costs do not exist if the firm is not doing business. Thus, by definition, variable costs are zero when no output is being produced. At that time, fixed costs are the only costs that will be incurred. Examples of variable

costs include cost of goods sold, factory labor, and sales commissions.

Break-even analysis will provide a sales objective that can be expressed in either dollars or units of production or sales, or whatever else is relevant. If the breakeven point is known, it can be a definite target to be reached and exceeded by carefully reasoned steps.

The basic breakeven equation is:

$$B/E = FC + VC$$
$$FC = \text{fixed costs in dollars}$$
$$VC = \text{variable costs in dollars}$$

Breakeven Equations

- B/E = FC + VC
- B/E S = FC /{I - (VC / S)}
- GM = GP / S

Key: B/E = Breakeven
FC = Total Fixed Costs in dollars
VC = Total Variable Costs in Dollars
S = Total Sales in Dollars
GM = Gross Margin
GP = Gross Profit (S – VC)

Variations on this basic formula can be used when different combinations of the basic factors are known, such as: B/E = FC/(1-VC/S), where FC = total fixed costs in dollars, VC = total variable costs in dollars, and S = total sales in dollars.

It is also possible to calculate your breakeven point when you do not sales know what your total variable cost will be, but you know your gross margin. The gross margin is the percentage of gross profit to sales (gross profit divided by).

The gross profit is the amount remaining once the variable costs have been subtracted from sales. This equation is B/E = FC/GM, and GM = GP/S, where FC = total fixed costs in dollars, GP = gross profit (or sales minus variable costs), and S = sales in total dollars.

Another way to calculate breakeven sales level is by using a breakeven chart. In constructing a breakeven chart, the vertical axis represents total dollars of activity, and the horizontal axis represents dollar or unit sales or some other measure of activity. Fixed costs are shown as a horizontal line, and variable costs are shown rising from the intersection of the fixed cost line with the vertical axis. As long as the sales price is greater than the variable costs, the sales line will eventually cross the variable cost line. The point of intersection of the sales line and the variable cost line represents the breakeven point.

Many people find a breakeven chart more useful than the more accurate number method used above, simply because of the visual aspect. With the breakeven chart, the relationships between the elements can be directly examined and experimented with to provide a better understanding of how the business works.

Any close decision will probably be affected by other factors in addition to these calculations anyway.

Breakeven helps to show the reasonableness of your Forecasts

Once you know the level of sales you have to reach before making a profit, you can evaluate the reasonableness of this target. What are the odds of reaching this breakeven sales level?

One way to test this is to convert the gross dollar sales needed for breakeven into some other unit, which can then be compared against the capacity of the business or the size of the market. If the breakeven occurs at or near the capacity of the business, or if your analysis shows that you must capture all (or more than all) of the available market, the feasibility of your concept is suspect, and the odds of business success are loaded against you.

Another way to use breakeven analysis is to change the variables in the equation. If fixed or variable expenses can be reduced, the breakeven point will go down. For example, if you can increase prices without hurting sales (and without increasing costs), the breakeven point will go down. This is an excellent way to experiment with different alternatives.

Clearly, this is a subjective process - but then, so is the rest of business analysis. The purpose is to make your business decision making as reasonable as possible. Breakeven analysis can be one of the most valuable tools at your disposal for this purpose.

Breakeven Chart

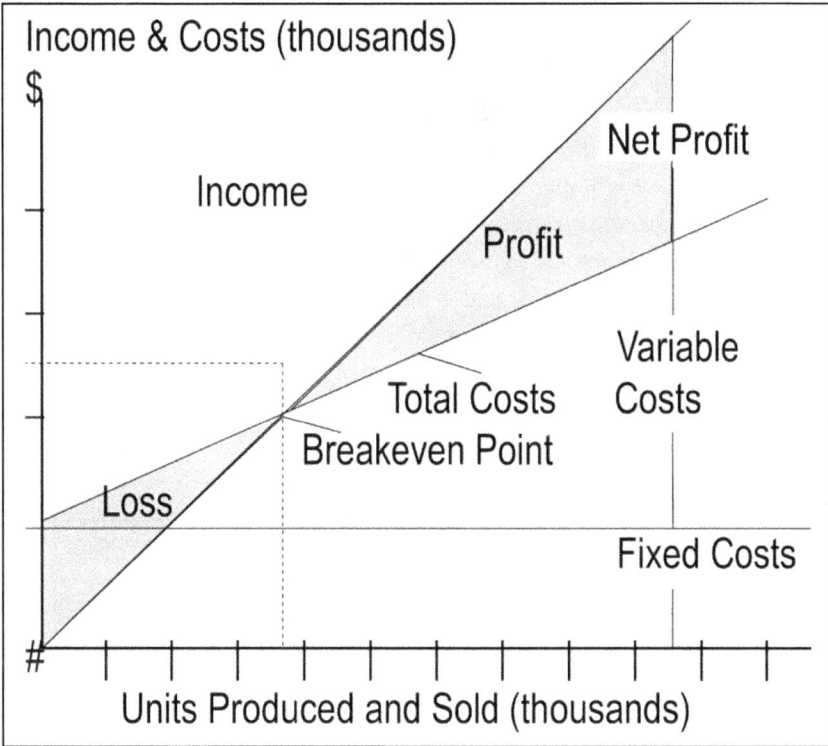

6c: Calculate Your Breakeven

Based on the information you have been assembling through the prior exercises, you can now calculate your breakeven point. As noted, breakeven is that point where the business neither makes a profit or a loss. The important point about breakeven is that if your sales are below your breakeven sales level, you WILL incur a loss!

You can experiment with the model to see how changes in any of the categories will change the breakeven target. Many times businesses think that lowering their price will increase their sales. This will let you determine the feasibility of lowering your price for example. It may be that the lower return per unit of sale produces a breakeven sales goal that is simply too large to meet in your present market. If that is the case, it would be a bad decision to lower your price. It is very interesting to play the "What If" game in this manner, and gives you some very valuable insight into how your business actually works.

Calculate Breakeven		
	Category	**Amount**
1	Unit Price	
2	Cost Per Unit	
3	Gross Profit Per Unit (Line 1 minus Line 2)	
4	Profit Margin (Line 3 divided by Line 1 as a decimal)	
5	Total Fixed Expenses (List Separately)	
6	Breakeven Sales Level Required (Line 5 divided by Line 4)	

Cash Flow Management

Cash - the organization's most precious asset. Control your cash before it controls you.

Cash flow management is a problem for almost any firm, large or small. The worst symptom of the problem: the business runs out of cash. Watching a business floundering, running out of cash even as it makes great sales and profits is painful. Painful though it may be, it is common and repeatedly the cause of business failure.

Small businesses are especially vulnerable to cash flow problems since they frequently operate with inadequate cash reserves or none at all and, worse, tend to miss the implications of negative cash flow until it's too late. However, even for larger organizations, the departmental budget is often as rigid - exceed your spending budget and you are out of business as well.

The Cash Flow Cycle
Cash flows through a business in different forms.

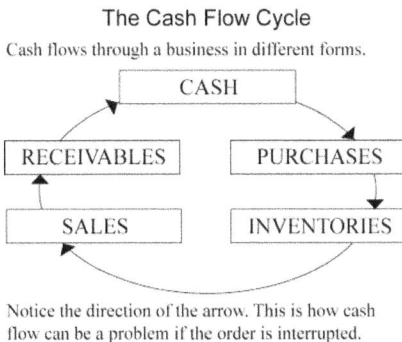

Notice the direction of the arrow. This is how cash flow can be a problem if the order is interrupted.

For financing purposes, cash flow projections are generally the most crucial aspect of the business plan. Bankers and other outside financing intermediaries will almost always look for a cash flow analysis in preference to any other financial statement, because this will show how the loan can be repaid.

In larger companies, the cash budget for a new project or expansion is critical to the overall decision to commit funds and move forward.

Why is cash flow so important? If the cash inflows exceed the cash outflows, the business can continue operations.

If the cash outflows exceed the inflows, the business RUNS OUT OF CASH and grinds to a halt. Even if the imbalance is only a short period, it can spell disaster.

In its simplest form, cash flow refers to the flows of cash, literally, into and out of the business. Think in terms of actual cash, dollar bills, flowing in and out of the business, and then identify both their sources and uses. This is cash-flow analysis.

TIMING and cash flow are inseparable. Suppliers typically expect payment often even before your customers pay their bills. As a result, the operation is very likely to have a negative cash flow when it grows dramatically. Periods of change are always reflected in an altered cash flow. If sales fall off, the cash flow slows down. Often, even if sales increase, the cash flow may stop completely or even become negative. Think of the impact of credit sales on cash flow, for example. One-time events such as changes in competition could trigger such consequences. More commonly, seasonal fluctuations may also pose cash flow problems where a build-up of inventories must precede the sales cycle (such as a toy business prior to the Christmas holidays.

Whatever the cause, the underlying message is simple: Run out of cash and the business is in trouble. Even if you can raise more money from other sources, sooner or later the timing of cash inflows must match the outflows if the business is to survive.

How to get cash flow under control? It's not easy. Some businesses never achieve cash flow control. These businesses are always in trouble, chronically overdrawn, slow in paying bills, and will eventually fold. They fold though, only after their owner/managers have spent a great deal of time worrying and probably spent all of their personal assets trying to cover the operating deficits. This kind of complication need not be an integral part of business management. Instead it is essential to PLAN and SCHEDULE so that cash flow for the business is positive.

Cash flow management does not need to be mysterious or complex. Managing cash is all about timing the inflows and outflows. Cash Flow Analysis starts the process. This can be as simple as going to your checkbook or accounting system and analyzing your receipts and disbursements over the past few months. A pattern is likely to emerge. What are the revenue sources, and how consistent are they from month to month? As well, what are the expenditures, and how repeatable are they from month to month? Next, look at the incoming revenue stream

(Accounts Receivable) or your sales forecast to confirm and further predict cash inflows, and your Accounts Payables to build a pattern of required future disbursements. Match the two. Is there a positive or negative cash flow?

If there is a negative cash flow, the deficit needs to be covered from somewhere. There are two options. Spend less, or get more (increase revenues). Even it the cash flow is positive, inspecting the individual elements may further improve operations. Are there cash inflows or outflows that can be changed?

Flows of Cash

INFLOWS
New Investment
New Debt
Sale of Fixed Assets
Operating Profits

OUT-FLOWS
Income Statement Expenses
Principal Portion of Loans

Cash inflows can be increased by adding new outside cash (usually a limited or one-time option) or, more commonly, by offering a discount for cash payments or for accelerated payments on regular accounts receivable (so-called "quick pays"). Another option for businesses normally offering open account credit (which become the Accounts Receivable) is to offer credit cards instead.

Today, many corporate customers, including many federal agencies, utilize credit cards for purchases to eliminate much internal paper work for themselves.

Cash outflows can often be reduced and/or delayed. They can be reduced by eliminating certain costs (Do you really need a … ?) They can frequently be delayed by negotiating or taking longer payment times than you have observed in the past. Many smaller businesses pay their monthly bills (their Accounts Payable) more quickly than they need to in an effort to maintain a good credit rating. The primary criterion here, however, is not necessarily how quickly you pay, but the consistency with which you pay. If you are inclined to pay bills at the end of the month in which they were received, instead, establish a policy to pay 30 or 40 days after receipt. You will automatically gain the equivalent of one to three weeks spending as a one-time improvement in your cash balances, and may be better able to align outflows (expenditures) with inflows (receipts).

Understand what your own cash flow cycle is. This process will take time and thought - otherwise it won't work. It is essential to take time to experiment with combinations of different alternatives. A controlled cash flow, the end result of this process, will more than repay the time and effort given to it. In fact, it may save the life of the business - and the future of the owner/managers as well.

Run your business - don't let it run you. This is COMMON SENSE.

6d: Financial Calculators

There are many online tools to help with a myriad of business calculations. The links shown here are representative and useful. Click or paste any of the links below to perform various financial analysis calculations to determine specific forecast figures. For a range of business calculations and other business worksheets, go to: http://www.buzgate.org/8.0/ca/ft.html.

- o Breakeven and Sales Analysis Worksheet
     http://www.buzgate.org/8.0/pdf/cs2_breakeven.pdf

- o Marginal Contribution Analysis Model – Excel Worksheet
     1. How many additional units must I sell to cover $_____ in additional costs?
     2. If I can make/sell _____ units per month, will I operate at a profit or a loss?
     http://www.buzgate.org/8.0/excel/Revenue-Units_Feasibility_Model.xls

- o Annual Forecasting Model – Excel Worksheet
     1. What will be my profitability given _____ level of sales?
     2. What is my breakeven?
     3. Play the "What If" game – change your assumptions, introduce new costs, or reductions – see the result on your breakeven
     http://www.buzgate.org/8.0/excel/forecasting_wrksht.xls

- o Cash Flow Analysis – An Excel Worksheet from SCORE
  1. How does offering/using credit affect my cash flow?
  http://www.buzgate.org/8.0/excel/cashflow_wrksht.xls

Free Online Calculators:

- o Calculate Breakeven
  (http://www.dinkytown.net/java/BreakEven.html)
- o Calculate Cash Flow
  (http://www.dinkytown.net/java/CashFlow.html)
- o Calculate Inventory Analysis
  (http://www.dinkytown.net/java/Inventory.html)
- o Calculate Profit Margin
  (http://www.dinkytown.net/java/ProfitMargin.html)
- o Calculate Working Capital
  (http://www.dinkytown.net/java/Capital.html)

Enter Answers from Calculators	
Breakeven	
Cash Flow	
Inventory Analysis	
Profit Margin	
Working Capital	

6e: Profit / Loss Forecast Worksheet

In 6a, you started a listing of the sources you expect to generate revenues from and a listing of expenses you felt you were likely to incur. In this worksheet, you will refine these rough numbers even more, based on what you have now learned about the forecasting process.

This exercise is designed to help you understand the forecasting process and to identify all of the revenues and expenses you are likely to incur. If there are other categories that are not listed, add them. If some categories do not pertain to your operation, ignore them. Be as inclusive as possible.

Profit / Loss Forecast Worksheet

Line	Revenue Categories	Projected	Example
1	Sales Revenues – Product 1 (Quantity x Unit Price)	$	$166,500.00
2	Sales Revenues – Product 2 (Quantity x Unit Price)		
3	Sales Revenues – Product 3 (Quantity x Unit Price)		
4	Sales Revenues – Product 4 (Quantity x Unit Price)		
5	Sales Revenues – Services (Hours x Price per Hour)		$ 12,300.00
6	Other Revenue Source(s)		$ 200.00
7	**Total Sales Revenues** (Total Line 1 through 6)	$	$179,000.00
	Expense Categories	**Projected**	**Example**
8	**I. Variable Costs** (Costs that change with levels of output/sales)		
9	Cost of Goods/Materials		$ 42,350.00
10	Direct Labor		$ 23,400.00
11	Payroll Taxes		$ 2,340.00
12	Production Facilities; electricity, heat, water, etc.		$ 1,800.00
13	Health Insurance		$ 4,200.00
14	Freight-In		$ 825.00
15	Truck Expense		$ 2,200.00
16	Equipment Maintenance		$ 750.00
17	Worker's Compensation Insurance		$ 100.00
18	Miscellaneous or Other		$ 65.00
19	**Total Variable Costs** (Total Line 9 through Line 18)	$	$ 78,030.00
20	**Gross Profit** (Line 7 minus Line 19)	$	$100,970.00
21	**II. Fixed Costs** (Not related to changes in output/sales)		
22	Administrative Salaries		$ 6,600.00
23	Owner's Compensation		$ 42,300.00
24	Payroll Taxes		$ 4,200.00
25	Health Insurance		$ 5,400.00
26	Rent (or Mortgage Interest)		$ 12,500.00
27	Other Interest		$ 750.00
28	Legal and Accounting		$ 1,650.00
29	Property Taxes		$ 1,875.00
30	Utilities (Power and Heat)		$ 540.00
31	Postage and Shipping		$ 750.00
32	General Insurance		$ 950.00
33	Office Supplies and Equipment		$ 1,350.00
34	Depreciation		$ 850.00
35	Telephone		$ 550.00
36	Travel		$ 1,350.00
37	Miscellaneous or Other		$ 250.00
38	**Total Fixed Costs** (Total Line 22 through Line 37)	$	$ 80,815.00
	Net Profit / Loss (Total Line 20 minus Line 38)	$	$ 20,155.00

6f: Strategic Mapping Worksheet

The Strategic Mapping Worksheet allows you to summarize your goals in a trackable format where the actions and decisions you make for tomorrow are in direct alignment with your longer term goals. This Worksheet brings about an alignment between the planning process and its implementation.

Using the data you have compiled through the different forecasting exercises earlier in this Step, complete the worksheet, extending these projections into a three year time frame.

STRATEGIC MAPPING WORKSHEET						
Projected & Actual Results	3 Year Goal	2 Year Goal	1 Year Goal	Present Year	Past Year	Past 2 Years
Sales						
Gross Margin						
Net Profit (EBIT)						
Breakeven						
Inventory						
Units Produced						
Units Sold						
Number of Customers						
Advertising Budget (% of Sales)						
Number of Employees						
Number of Locations						
Place a checkmark for the following where applicable						
Geographic Penetration						
Local						
Regional						
National						
International						
Internet Presence						
Website						
E-Commerce Site						
Other Factors						

Forecast Counseling

There are many public sector resources that exist to help small businesses is various ways. We have directed you to the BUZGate Resource Network in earlier Steps to locate appropriate resources to provide you with additional help.

Each state has a Small Business Development Center (SBDC) network, cosponsored with the US Small Business Administration and state-based college or university system. These SBDCs employ professional counselors who provide guidance to small businesses at no charge. SCORE is another counseling network where experienced business executives volunteer their time to assist smaller companies at no cost.

To access this information, use this link: www.BUZGate.org, then click on your state, then click on Free Help. Select the Business Counseling category.

Summary Step 6

In this Step the goal is to build a financial model of how the business will operate, showing where revenues will come from and what costs will be incurred to support those revenue streams. Using the approach developed earlier in this section, you can calculate your breakeven and so have a realistic picture of the feasibility of the business operation.

Instructions: Fill in the data from your earlier work. There are no right or wrong answers. Think about your answers and talk them over with someone else – your partner, mentor or counselor. Using this as a basis for discussion can often uncover other issues affecting the business development process.

Financial Forecasting		
	Category	$$$
1	Total Projected Revenue	
2	Total Variable Costs	
3	Gross Profit (Line 1 minus Line 2)	
4	Profit Margin (Line 3 divided by Line 1 as %)	
5	Total Fixed Expenses	
6	Net Profit / Loss (Line 3 minus Line 5)	
7	Breakeven (Line 5 divided by Line 4)	
8	Working Capital (Current Assets minus Current Liabilities)	

Here are the interesting questions:

o   Does your operation show a profit?

o   Is your gross margin in line with your industries standards?

o   Do you understand what factors affect your breakeven? What makes it go up? Or go down?

o   What factors affect your working capital?

Now on to Step 7...

7

Financing

Am I aware of my business financing needs?

In this Section:

- o   Introduction
- o   Cash Needs
    - o   Assets
    - o   Working Capital
    - o   Contingency Reserve
- o   The Financing Proposal
    - o   Short term, Intermediate term and long term financing
- o   Why Forecast?
- o   Funding Support / Sources
- o   Financial Counseling
- o   Exercises:
    - o   Financial Planning Worksheet
    - o   Personal Financial Analysis
    - o   Financial Sources Worksheet
    - o   Financial Calculators
    - o   Summary Step 7

Step 7

Financing

Introduction

Three things determine the amount of financing you will need to start your business:

- o The amount you need to spend on "assets" or the equipment, tools, computers, or other tangible things you need to operate your business;

- o The amount of "working capital" you must have available; and

- o A "contingency reserve" you should have available in case things don't work out quite as fast as you hoped.

There is a very specific way these costs are determined.

Cash Needs

Assets = $$$$???
Working Capital = $$$$???
Contingency Reserve = $$$$???

Your assets are generally the easiest to identify. Simply make a list of what you will need – then check with professionals in your field to see what you might have missed.

Your working capital needs are determined from your Cash Flow forecast (Step 6). Your contingency needs are determined from your cash flow by making a "worst case" forecast, and looking at the extended working capital needs that would be generated by this event.

Once you have determined how much financing you will need, you can start the process of locating the "right" type of financing for each need. There are many sources to research ranging from banks to various federal, state, regional and local financing programs. A qualified financial counselor or consultant can be very helpful in identifying and approaching the "right" financing sources.

In this step, you will use a worksheet to identify how much financing you may need, and then evaluate different sources that may be available to you to locate the "right' financing for your needs. You can get help from your local SBDC, SCORE, MicroCredit or local banker.

Step 7 Components:

- o   Financing Proposal Article
- o   Financial Planning Worksheet
- o   SBA Loan Programs
- o   Business / Personal Financial Statement
- o   Financial Calculators
- o   Links To Resources For Financing

The Financing Proposal

The traditional business plan format typically requires few alternations to also serve as a first-rate financing proposal. There are some areas of your plan that will be of little or no use to prospective financiers. Personal histories, for example, can and should be replaced by resumes. The business plan section on deviation analysis would typically not be required as well. This is an internal control process and one not normally useful to outsiders. The main difference between your business plan and financing proposal lies in the fact that while the main function of the plan is to enable you to understand the complexities of the business, the function of a financing proposal is to show your prospective backers that you not only know what you are doing, but will also be able to make their investment as risk free as possible.

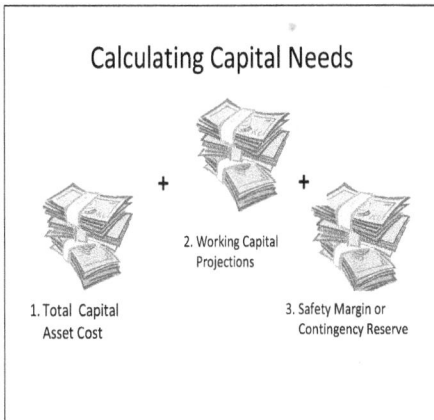

Calculating Capital Needs

1. Total Capital Asset Cost
2. Working Capital Projections
3. Safety Margin or Contingency Reserve

As you begin to establish your financing strategy for your new venture, it is important to be aware of different sources and types. The use of an Analytical Financing Chart (next section) will help you to determine your financing needs, types, and sources. Venture capital or other forms of higher-risk capital represent ways many high technology ventures have been financed over the past decade.

More conventional forms of entrepreneurial financing, such as bank loans and other institutional credit-based services, have consistently served the smaller business venture. In each situation, however, assessing the longer-term viability of the business concept is equally important to the lender.

Although the greatest dollar amounts of financing for many smaller businesses are found in trade credit (that is, money owed to suppliers), the most important single financing source is your local bank.

Such esoteric financing tools as factoring or discounting receivables, bonds, convertible debentures, and other such debt instruments are typically not utilized by smaller businesses. If you have need of them, your banker and accountant can help you. If you do not have both a banker and an accountant, you surely have no need of specialized financing and probably should reconsider going into business at all.

In seeking financing, it is essential to recognize the difference between debt and equity. When you go to a bank, you are seeking "debt money," a loan that you repay over a period of time at a certain additional cost of interest.

Three Types of Lending

1. **Short Term Financing**
   - Financing, usually through notes, to be paid within one year of less, and pain in one sum.

2. **Intermediate Term Financing**
   - Funding for one to five years, usually repaid on a monthly basis.

3. **Long Term Financing**
   - Financing for five or more years, such as real estate financing, where repayment is make on a schedule over a period of time

The money you and others invest in the venture is ordinarily "equity," that is, money invested in a business that will not be repaid unless the ownership rights that it represents are sold to another. Debt financing does not lead to sharing ownership of your business with the financier; equity financing does.

" Control" is another matter: Your banker or some other lender frequently exercises substantial control over a business through various legal documents (for example, agreements not to further borrow, working capital maintenance, cash reserves) or through suggestion but still does not own a share of the venture. Debt pays interest, usually for a finite period; equity pays (shares) profits forever.

The distinction between debt and equity is of particular interest to a banker because the more debt there is in relation to equity (that is, the greater the "leverage"), normally the higher the risk. A high debt-to-worth ratio (worth is roughly equivalent to equity but includes certain kinds of specialized debt) indicates high risk. High risk costs money, if indeed money can be found for such a situation. Why? Because debt money is rented money, and the rent must be paid no matter what the business is doing. A higher than normal debt service obligation requires that a business perform better than normal just to meet this additional demand. Very simply, if you can't meet your debt payment, you go out of business.

The problem here is important. Sometimes entrepreneurs, having read books on getting rich using other people's money, will find so much debt financing that they can never get ahead no matter how hard they work. Without capital (that is, permanent, non-repayable money invested in the business) they may spin their wheels forever, a problem known as "overtrading." The trade ratios of sales/worth are guidelines to follow. References to these and other valuable business planning data may be found at http://www.bizbound.com/listof.html.

Risk Assessment

Whenever anyone considers how to finance a business, the phrase "risk assessment" or some variation is likely to be discussed. Since the criteria on which risk is judged vary from business principal to banker, and you know what risk looks like from your own point of view, it may be helpful to look at risk from a banker's point of view. After all, you wouldn't be applying for financing unless you thought the risk was reasonable. The test of reasonableness is the benefit from the use of borrowed money weighed against the potential cost, cost frequently being a function of risk. Your conclusions about "reasonableness" or "risk" should not be based on "hunch" or "gut feeling" but should be the result of a systematic analysis.

In assessing the risk level of a loan, a banker will generally consider at least the following:

1. Experience of the borrower: A new business is more risky than an established business. A newcomer to an industry has more danger for a banker than a well-seasoned practitioner. Experience is one of the best business teachers. Without it, some typically expensive lessons are all but inevitable.

2. Experience with the borrower: The credit history of the individuals in a small company is important because loans to small businesses are, in essence, personal loans, whether they are secured or unsecured. The "character" of a person is shown with some accuracy by that person's track record. Your banker will want to know yours.

3. Ability of the borrower to pay back the loan: This is actually the single most important consideration, but it cannot be made in a vacuum. Such factors as your experience, character, the industry's cycle, and the period of the loan will all affect this part of the judgment. Your cash flow will show how the loan will be repaid. This must be clearly shown for any loan application.

4. Equity in the business: The greater the equity, the lower the risk. Bankers as a rule like to see a very low debt-to-worth ratio. Equity has a tendency to make people stick with their business more when it becomes troubled.

5. Collateral, cosigners, and co-makers: All of these reduce the risk, but, except for some finance companies, the coverage afforded by these is less important than the fact that they are tangible evidence of others' faith in your business.

6. Term of the loan: The longer the term, the higher the risk. On the other side, the shorter the term, the lower the risk. If you don't pay back a thirty-day note, your banker knows it fast. A twenty-year loan may not show problems until it is too late to cure them.

Risk assessment affects you in two direct ways. First, in whether you get the financing or not and second, how much the financing will cost you. By presenting your case in the best light, either through a financing plan or through a combination of plan, experience and updated statements, you enhance your chances of getting the money you need and getting it at the lowest cost.

Exercises Step 7: Financing

7a. Financial Planning Worksheet

7b. Personal Financial Analysis

7c. Financial Sources Worksheet

7d. Financial Calculators

7e. Summary Step 7

Now on to the exercises......

7a: Financial Planning Worksheet

There are a variety of reasons that a business requires financing including initial capital assets, start-up cash flow needs, seasonal cash flow fluctuations, and cash demands from growth. The following worksheet will help you begin to identify the different amounts of financing you will need for your own venture, and appropriate potential sources to secure funding.

Complete the following worksheet with the best information you have available at this time. You can always come back later to update this information.

Financial Planning Worksheet
Start-Up Phase
Organizational Expenses (Check all that apply)
1. Funding for fees such as business filings, etc.　　　　Amount $_____
❑ Personal Funds ❑ Family Funds ❑ Partners ❑ Private Investors ❑ Second Mortgage ❑ Not Apply ❑ Other (Explain)
2. Funding for deposit requirements such as rent, utilities, etc　　Amount $_____
❑ Personal Funds ❑ Family Funds ❑ Partners ❑ Private Investors ❑ Second Mortgage ❑ Not Apply ❑ Other (Explain)
3. Funding for regulatory requirements such as licenses, permits, etc.　Amount $_____
❑ Personal Funds ❑ Family Funds ❑ Partners ❑ Private Investors ❑ Second Mortgage ❑ Not Apply ❑ Other (Explain)
4. Other organizational funding needs (Specify) _____　　Amount $_____
❑ Personal Funds ❑ Family Funds ❑ Partners ❑ Private Investors ❑ Second Mortgage ❑ Not Apply ❑ Other (Explain)
Inventories (Check all that apply)
5. Funding for initial inventories such as parts, shipping materials, etc.　Amount $_____
❑ Personal Funds ❑ Family Funds ❑ Partners ❑ Private Investors ❑ Second Mortgage ❑ Not Apply ❑ Other (Explain)
Capital Expenditures (Check all that apply)
6. Funding for production facilities, real estate, etc.　　　Amount $_____
❑ Personal Funds ❑ Family Funds ❑ Partners ❑ Private Investors ❑ Second Mortgage ❑ Not Apply ❑ Other (Explain)
7. Funding for equipment such as machines, computers, etc.　　Amount $_____
❑ Personal Funds ❑ Family Funds ❑ Partners ❑ Private Investors ❑ Second Mortgage ❑ Not Apply ❑ Other (Explain)
8. Funding for fixtures such as lighting, shelving, alarm systems, etc.　Amount $_____
❑ Personal Funds ❑ Family Funds ❑ Partners ❑ Private Investors ❑ Second Mortgage ❑ Not Apply ❑ Other (Explain)

© Knowledge Institute

Financial Planning Worksheet (Continued)
9. Other capital expenditure funding needs (Specify)_____ Amount $_____
❑ Personal Funds ❑ Family Funds ❑ Partners ❑ Private Investors ❑ Second Mortgage ❑ Not Apply ❑ Other (Explain)
Working Capital (Check all that apply)
10. Funding for initial working capital (Sum negative cash flows to breakeven) Amount $_____
❑ Personal Funds ❑ Family Funds ❑ Partners ❑ Private Investors ❑ Second Mortgage ❑ Not Apply ❑ Other (Explain)
Seasonal Phase
Seasonal Expenditures (Check all that apply)
11. Funding for seasonal inventory   Amount $_____
❑ Secured Short-Term Loan   ❑ Unsecured Short-Term Loan ❑ Line of Credit ❑ Accounts Receivable Financing ❑ Credit Cards   ❑ Not Apply ❑ Other (Explain)
12. Funding for seasonal accounts receivable   Amount $_____
❑ Secured Short-Term Loan   ❑ Unsecured Short-Term Loan ❑ Line of Credit ❑ Accounts Receivable Financing ❑ Credit Cards   ❑ Not Apply ❑ Other (Explain)
13. Funding for seasonal marketing   Amount $_____
❑ Secured Short-Term Loan   ❑ Unsecured Short-Term Loan ❑ Line of Credit ❑ Accounts Receivable Financing ❑ Credit Cards   ❑ Not Apply ❑ Other (Explain)
14. Funding for seasonal payroll   Amount $_____
❑ Secured Short-Term Loan   ❑ Unsecured Short-Term Loan ❑ Line of Credit ❑ Accounts Receivable Financing ❑ Credit Cards   ❑ Not Apply ❑ Other (Explain)
15. Funding for seasonal supplies   Amount $_____
❑ Secured Short-Term Loan   ❑ Unsecured Short-Term Loan ❑ Line of Credit ❑ Accounts Receivable Financing ❑ Credit Cards   ❑ Not Apply ❑ Other (Explain)
16. Funding for seasonal working capital   Amount $_____
❑ Secured Short-Term Loan   ❑ Unsecured Short-Term Loan ❑ Line of Credit ❑ Accounts Receivable Financing ❑ Credit Cards   ❑ Not Apply ❑ Other (Explain)
17. Funding for other seasonal expenditures (Specify)_____ Amount $_____
❑ Secured Short-Term Loan   ❑ Unsecured Short-Term Loan ❑ Line of Credit ❑ Accounts Receivable Financing ❑ Credit Cards   ❑ Not Apply ❑ Other (Explain)

© Knowledge Institute

Funding Support / Sources

There are a variety of ways to fund a new business or raise funds for an ongoing business concern. These include both subsidized public agency programs, as well as private sector options.

Sources of Financing

- Your Savings
- Your Family
- Your Friends
- Business Profits
- Trade Credit
- Banking Institutions
- Professional Investor
- Public Programs

Most funding for a new venture is provided by the entrepreneur / business developers themselves, and comes from their savings and other personal resources, and from their family and friends. Traditionally, the next level is from their local bank in the form of a bank loan.

In the public arena, the U.S. Small Business Administration (SBA) represents a government agency that offers a variety of programs that foster increased lending to small businesses. There are also a variety of regional and local programs that fund business ventures that offer such specific benefits as the creation of new jobs and related community enhancements.

Private sector funding sources include Angel investors, venture capital firms and a wide variety of alternative funding options that support both startup and growth objectives. All of these programs may be found at www.BUZGate.org, select your state, then Free Help.

SBA Loan Programs

The SBA offers numerous loan programs to assist small businesses. It is important to note, however, that the SBA is primarily a guarantor of loans made by private and other institutions. Go to the SBA website to learn more about the following (www.SBA.gov):

7(a) Loan Guaranty Program

The 7(a) Loan Guaranty Program is one of the SBA's primary lending programs for businesses that might not be eligible for business loans through normal lending channels. The program operates through private-sector lenders, primarily banks, which issue loans that are, in turn, guaranteed by the SBA. Loan proceeds can be used for most sound business purposes including working capital, machinery and equipment, furniture and fixtures, land and building (including purchase, renovation and new construction), leasehold improvements, and debt refinancing (under special conditions). Loan maturity is up to 10 years for working capital and generally up to 25 years for fixed assets.

Microloan 7(m) Loan Program

The Microloan 7(m) Loan Program was developed to increase the availability of small loans to prospective small business borrowers by providing short-term loans of up to $35,000 to small businesses and not-for-profit child-care centers for working capital or the purchase of inventory, supplies, furniture, fixtures, machinery and/or equipment.

Patriot Express Loan

Launched in June of 2007, this pilot loan initiative is targeted toward veterans and members of the military community who want to establish or expand a small business. Contact your local bank to inquire if they provide loans that are guaranteed by the SBA Patriot Express 7(a) Loan Program.

Disadvantaged Business Enterprise (DBE)

Any business that is majority owned, operated, and controlled by a citizen of the United States, or lawfully admitted permanent resident, that is Black, Hispanic, Native Americans, Asian-Pacific Islanders, Subcontinent Asians, or women regardless of race, may consider becoming a certified Disadvantaged Business Enterprise (DBE) in order to become eligible for doing business with government agencies and hundreds of national corporations who are looking to specifically do business with DBEs. To become certified, you will need to complete a Uniform Disadvantaged Business Enterprise (DBE) Application.

Small Business Investment Company (SBIC)

An SBIC is a privately owned and managed venture capital firm that is licensed and regulated by the SBA. SBICs are located across the country and use a combination of funds raised from private sources and through the use of SBA guarantees to make equity and mezzanine capital investments in small businesses.

CDC - 504 Loans

The 504 Certified Development Company (CDC) Program provides growing businesses with long-term, fixed-rate financing for major fixed assets, such as land and buildings. A CDC is a nonprofit corporation set up to contribute to the economic development of its community or region. CDCs work with the SBA and private-sector lenders to provide financing to small businesses. There are about 290 CDCs nationwide.

SBA Export Working Capital Program (EWCP)

EWCP Loans are targeted for businesses that are able to generate export sales and need additional working capital in the form of transaction financing to support these sales. The SBA delivers its export loan program through a network of SBA Senior International Credit Officers located in US Export Assistance Centers throughout the country.

SBA CAPLines Loan Program

Short term loans and revolving lines of credit designed to support small business short-term and cyclical working capital needs. There are five types of CAPLine Programs: Seasonal Line, Contract Line, Builders Line, Standard Asset-Based and Small Asset-Based Lines.

Business Stabilization Program

As part of America's Recovery and Reinvestment Act of 2009, the SBA is offering loans to businesses that already have a bank-issued loan. The business can borrow up to $35,000 to make interest payments and pay down principal on existing debt up to six months. The loan is essentially interest free with no repayment for a year and full repayment in five years. Contact your local bank to learn if they are issuing this type of loan as the SBA will fully subsidize the interest and 100% guarantee the loan making it very attractive for the bank to work with you.

SBA Disaster Loan

If you are in a declared disaster area and are the victim of a disaster, you may be eligible for financial assistance from the U.S. Small Business Administration - even if you don't own a business. As a homeowner, renter and/or personal-property owner, you may apply to the SBA for a loan to help you recover from a disaster.

SBA Loan FAQs

Visit the SBA website and click on Starting and Managing a Business to learn how an SBA Loan Program works and where to apply.

Federal Grant Resources

SBA Grant programs generally support nonprofit organizations, intermediary lending institutions, and state and local governments in an effort to expand and enhance small business technical and financial assistance. The SBA does not offer grants to start or expand small businesses.

Vocational Rehabilitation

Specialized financial support may be available to individuals who qualify for support through state-based Vocational Rehabilitation programs and, at the national level, through veteran-oriented Vocational Rehabilitation programs. Check with your Vocational Rehabilitation counselor to determine what you may qualify for.

Other Financing Programs

There are a plethora of other programs at the Federal, state and local level. These programs are listed in www.BUZGate.org. Go to BUZGate, click on your state, select Free Help, and select Financing Programs.

Financing – A 6 Step Approach

1. Identify different needs for funds within the business
   a. Capital Assets
   b. Working Capital
   c. Contingency Reserve

2. Determine how much money is needed in each category
   a. Look to your projections

3. Identify the type of money needed (Financial Sources Worksheet)
   a. Short Term Debt (Secured / Unsecured)
   b. Trade Credit
   c. Lease vs. Purchase
   d. Line of Credit
   e. Long Term Debt
   f. Sale of Stock

4. Schedule when money is needed
   a. Timing is critical – don't finance more than you need

5. Develop a financing plan
   a. The financing proposal is a sub-set of the business plan

6. Implement and review your financing plan
   a. Control = Monitor and Adjust

7b: Personal Financial Analysis Worksheet

Banks and other lenders will require much of the same information when you apply for financing. Even though you are a business entity seeking financing, they will almost certainly look to your personal financial position and history as an important part of any lending decision, and will also almost always ask you to personally guaranty any business debt. The worksheet on the following pages is typical of the personal financial statements you may be asked to complete. The wisdom is to be prepared.

Use the Personal Financial Analysis form to organize your personal and financial information in a similar way as may be required by a financial institution when applying for a business loan. The Form is printed on the next three pages to show what is required. You may copy and use this form, or use the following link to a PDF version that you can print out and have available when asked by lenders to provide this information:
http://www.buzgate.org/content/pdf/financial_statement.pdf.

Personal Financial Statement as of ___/___/___
Submitted to: (Name of lending institution)

This form introduces many of the components required for commercial lending transactions. Actual form categories may vary slightly relative to intended use and must comply with applicable laws & regulations.

APPLICANT (NAME)	CO-APPLICANT (NAME)
Employer Name_____	Employer _____
Address _____	Address_____
Phone Yrs. Employed Title/Position	Phone Yrs. Employed Title/Position
_____ _____ _____	_____ _____ _____
Prior Employer (if above < 3 yrs.) Yrs. Employed	Prior Employer (if above < 3 yrs.) Yrs. Employed
_____ _____	_____ _____
Home Address_____	Home Address_____
Phone SS# Date of Birth	Phone SS# Date of Birth
_____ _____ _____	_____ _____ _____
Accountant Name/Phone_____	Accountant Name/Phone_____
Attorney Name/Phone_____	Attorney Name/Phone_____
Investment Advisor Name/Phone_____	Investment Advisor Name/Phone_____
Insurance Advisor Name/Phone_____	Insurance Advisor Name/Phone_____

Cash Income & Expenditures Statement for Year Ended ___/___/___

ANNUAL INCOME	AMOUNT	ANNUAL EXPENDITURES	AMOUNT
Salary (applicant)	$_____	Federal Income and Other Taxes	$_____
Salary (co-applicant)	_____	State Income and Other Taxes	_____
Bonus/Commissions (applicant)	_____	Rent, Co-op, or Condo Fees	_____
Bonus/Commissions (co-applicant)	_____	Mortgage. (residential)	_____
Rental Income	_____	Property Taxes (residential)	_____
Interest Income	_____	Loans (interest & principal)	_____
Dividend Income	_____	Insurance (disability, medical, etc.)	_____
Capital Gains	_____	Investments (including tax shelters)	_____
Partnership Income	_____	Alimony/Child Support	_____
Other Investment Income	_____	Tuition	_____
Other Income (List)**	_____	Other Living Expense	_____
		Medical Expenses	_____
		Other Expense (List)	_____
Total Income	$_____	**Total Expenses**	$_____

Are significant changes projected over next 12 months? __Yes __No (If yes, attach information)
**Income from alimony, child support, or separate maintenance income need not be revealed if the applicant or co-applicant does not wish to have it considered as a basis for repaying this obligation.

Balance Sheet as of ___/___/___ ("s" LETTER - See Key on next page)

ASSETS	AMOUNT ($)	LIABILITIES	AMOUNT ($)
Cash (this institution)	$_____	Notes Payable	$_____
Cash (other institutions)	_____	Secured –	_____
Readily Marketable Securities (sA)	_____	Unsecured –	_____
Non-readily Marketable Securities (sA)	_____	Notes Payable to Others (sE)	_____
Accounts/Notes Receivable	_____	Secured –	_____
Net Cash Value of Life Ins. (sB)	_____	Unsecured –	_____
Residential Real Estate (sC)	_____	Accounts payable (i.e., credit cards)	_____
Real Estate Investments (sC)	_____	Margin Accounts	_____
Partnerships/PC Interests (sD)	_____	Notes Due: Partnership (sD)	_____
IRA, Keogh, Profit-sharing & Other Vested		Taxes Payable	_____
Retirement accounts	_____	Mortgage Debt (sC)	_____
Deferred Income (# of years __)	_____	Life Insurance Loans (sB)	_____
Personal Property (i.e., auto)	_____	Other Liabilities (list):	_____
Other Assets (list):	_____	**Total Liabilities:**	$_____
		Net Worth:	$_____
Total Assets:	$_____	**Combined Total:**	$_____

CONTINGENT LIABILITIES	YES	NO
Are you a guarantor, co-maker, or endorser for any debt of an individual, corporation, or partnership?	___	___
Do you have any outstanding letters of credit or surety bonds?	___	___
Are there any suits or legal actions pending against you?	___	___
Are you contingently liable on any lease or contract?	___	___
Are any of your tax obligations past due?	___	___

What would be your total estimated tax liability if you were to sell your major assets?
If yes for any of the above, provide details: _____

Key: Balance Sheet Section references to "s" where "s" refers to Schedule

Schedule A (sA) – All Securities (Including non-money market mutual funds)
For both readily marketable securities (including U.S. Governments and municipals) and non-readily marketable securities (closely held, thinly traded or restricted stock), provide number of shares (stock) or face value (bonds), description, owner(s), location held, cost, current market value, and pledged status (yes or no).

Schedule B (sB) – Insurance
Provide name of life insurance carrier, face amount and type of policy, beneficiary, cash surrender value, amount borrowed, and ownership of each policy applicable. List disability insurance in terms of monthly distribution and number of years covered for both applicant and co-applicant.

Schedule C (sC) – Personal Residence & Real Estate Investments, Mortgage Debt (majority ownership only**)**
For both personal residence and investment real estate, provide property address, legal owner, purchase year and price, market value, present loan balance, interest rate, loan maturity date, monthly payment, and name of lender.

Schedule D (sD) – Partnership (less than majority ownership for real estate partnerships)
For both business/professional and other investments (i.e., tax shelters) provide name and type of investment, date of initial investment, cost, percent owned, current market value, balance due on partnerships (notes, cash call) and final contribution date. For investments that represent a material portion of your total assets, include the relevant financial statements or tax returns or in the case of partnership investments or S-corporations, schedule K-1's.

Schedule E (sE) – Notes Payable
Provide due to, type of facility, amount of line, secured status (yes or no), collateral, interest rate, maturity, and unpaid balance.

Common Additional Questions:
- Income tax returns filed through (date): _____ Are any returns currently being audited or contested? __Y __N If yes, what year(s)?
- Have (either of) you or any firm in which you were a major owner ever declared bankruptcy? __Y __N If yes, provide details:
- Have you drawn a will? __Y __N If yes, please furnish the name of the executor(s) and year will was drawn:
- Number of dependants (excluding self) and relationship to applicant:
- Have you ever had a financial plan prepared for you? __Y __N
- Did you include two years federal and state tax returns with this form? __Y __N
- Do (either of) you have a line of credit or unused credit facility at any other institution(s)? __Y __N If so, indicate where, how much and name of financial institution:
- Do you anticipate any substantial inheritances? __Y __N If yes, explain:

Representations and Warranties
The information contained in this statement is provided to induce you to extend or to continue the extension of credit to the undersigned or to others upon the guarantee of the undersigned. The undersigned acknowledge and understand that you are relying on the information provided herein in deciding to grant or continue credit or to accept a guarantee thereof. Each of the undersigned represents, warrants and certifies that the information provided herein is true, correct and complete. Each of the undersigned agrees to notify you immediately and in writing of any change in name, address, or employment and of any ability of any of the undersigned to perform its (or their) obligations to you. In the absence of such notice or a new and full written statement, this should be considered as a continuing statement and substantially correct. If the undersigned fail to notify you as required above, or if any of the information herein should prove to be inaccurate or incomplete in any material respect, you may declare the indebtedness of the undersigned or the indebtedness guaranteed by the undersigned, as the case may be, immediately due and payable. You are authorized to make all inquiries you deem necessary to verify the accuracy of the information contained herein and to determine the credit-worthiness of the undersigned. The undersigned authorizes any person or consumer reporting agency to give you any information it may have on the undersigned. Each of the undersigned authorizes you to answer questions about your credit experience with the undersigned. As long as any obligation or guarantee of the undersigned to you is outstanding, the undersigned shall supply annually an updated financial statement. This personal financial statement and any other financial or other information that the undersigned give you shall be your property.

Date: ___/___/___   Your Signature: _____
Date: ___/___/___   Co-Applicant's Signature:_____
(if you are requesting the financial accommodation jointly)
This form is also available online at http://www.buzgate.org/content/pdf/financial_statement.pdf

7c. Financial Sources Worksheet

As we have noted earlier, different financing needs are supported by different forms of financing. The Financial Sources Worksheet allows you to identify the most appropriate form of financing to support your proposed use. It may be necessary to become very creative in forming your financing plan. You may be able to postpone some of your initial purchases, lease rather than buy, or use trade credit to help support your initial operations.

The real key, though, is to make sure that your business model really works before you enter into any type of financial obligations.

Can you actually sell your product or service to some customer?

7c: Financial Sources Worksheet

	Equity						Long Term Debt		Intermediate-Term Debt	Short Term Debt							Profits
	Personal	Family	Partners	Private Investors	Second Mortgage	Other	Mortgage	Secured L/T Loan		Secured S/T Loan	Unsecured S/T Loan	Line of Credit	Credit Cards	A/R Factoring	Leasing	Floor Planning	
Start-Up Costs																	
Organizational																	
Legal																	
Deposits																	
Other																	
Initial Inventories																	
Capital Expenditures																	
Plant / Real Estate																	
Equipment																	
Fixtures																	
Initial Working Capital																	
Other																	
Growth																	
Inventory																	
Accounts Receivable																	
Working Capital																	
Physical Improvements																	
Other																	
Seasonal																	
Inventory																	
Accounts Receivable																	
Marketing																	
Payroll																	
Supplies																	
Working Capital																	
Other																	

Examples of Sources of Funds:

1. Owners, relatives, friends
2. Private Investors
3. Trade Credit
4. Customers
5. Profits
6. Commercial Banks
7. Savings Banks
8. Commercial Credit Companies
9. Leasing Companies
10. Finance Companies
11. Life Insurance Companies
12. Small Business Administration
13. Small Business Investment Co. (SBIC)
14. Local Development Co. (LDC)
15. Regional Development Co. (RDC)
16. Consumer Finance Companies
17. State-based Programs – BF
18. Federal Programs - SBIR

7d: Financial Calculators

We provided these calculators in Step 6 also. With your further work in this Step 7, you ideas and assumptions may have changed. Use any of the links below to perform various financial analysis calculations to determine specific forecast figures.

Calculate Breakeven
(http://www.dinkytown.net/java/BreakEven.html)

Calculate Cash Flow
(http://www.dinkytown.net/java/CashFlow.html)

Calculate Inventory Analysis
(http://www.dinkytown.net/java/Inventory.html)

Calculate Profit Margin
(http://www.dinkytown.net/java/ProfitMargin.html)

Calculate Working Capital
(http://www.dinkytown.net/java/Capital.html)

Enter Answers from Calculators	
Breakeven	
Cash Flow	
Inventory Analysis	
Profit Margin	
Working Capital	

Summary Step 7

The goal in this Step is to develop an understanding of how much financing you will need to properly launch your venture, and where this financing might come from. In your eventual business plan / proposal, this information will be presented in a "Sources and Uses of Funds" section.

Fill in the data from your earlier work:

Uses & Sources of Funds	
Financing Uses	
Requirements	$$
Capital Investments	
Start-Up Phase	
Inventories	
Working Capital	
Seasonal	
Total Uses	$
Financing Sources	
Personal Funds	
Family Funds	
Partners	
Private Investors	
Second Mortgage	
Other	
Total Sources	$

STEP 8

Resource
Networks

Do I understand what assistance may be available from public agencies and private resources?

In this Section:

- o Introduction
- o Networking
- o Building Your Resource Networks
- o Exercises:
  - o US Small Business Administration
  - o Banking
  - o Schools and Colleges
  - o Professional Services / Accounting
  - o Professional Services / Legal
  - o Professional Services / Insurance
  - o Business Incubator
  - o BUZGate.org
  - o Summary Step 8

Step 8

Resource Networks

Introduction

Often it is the relationships and networks that help a business to succeed. This Step is an opportunity to identify important resources that you can start networking with to build awareness of other resources and your own support networks. As with earlier Steps, you will get as much out of these exercises as you put in. Our advice is to find these resources and then proactively build your networks. Here we provide listings of public sector agencies that can help with a variety of business development issues. There are private-sector partners that you will need to incorporate in your resource network as well. Ask business counselors for referrals or check with local business organizations such as the chamber of commerce.

Networking

Invest the time in building your Networks

It will repay you many times over

The activities in this Step are fieldwork. Start to identify your Resource Network partners – our BUZGate network will show you who they are and where they are located – then go and have a meeting with them.

Document the results of the meetings in building your Resource Network database. You will then not only know who to turn to for advice and support, but you can use these networks to build your business – relationships are everything!

Your time invested in this way will pay huge dividends.

Exercises Step 8: Resource Networks

8a. US Small Business Administration

8b. Banking

8c. Schools and Colleges

8d. Professional Services

8e. Business Incubator

8f. BUZGate.org

8g. Summary Step 8

Now on to the exercises…

Building Your Resource Network – Using the Worksheets

There are literally thousands of business assistance programs paid for with your tax dollars, available in every state. The Knowledge Institute's Business Utility Zone Gateway is a small business resource community listing thousands of free and low cost public programs available to help small businesses to get started and grow. These public assistance agencies exist to help you with various aspects of your business objectives. You will find an alphabetical listing for your state and organized by town of the organizations and people that are available to help you develop an appropriate action strategy. To find the agencies in your area, use this link: www.BUZGate.org, then click on your state, then click on Free Help. Select the category that best suits your need.

Each of the following worksheet pages lists a type of resource and provides a format for you to enter information you gained through an actual visit to that organization. Complete the worksheets as noted and you will be building a very valuable resource network.

8a. US Small Business Administration Resource Networks

The US Small Business Administration (SBA) offers financing, training, and advocacy for small firms. The SBA has offices in every state, including the District of Columbia, the Virgin Islands, and Puerto Rico. In addition, the SBA works with thousands of lending, educational and training institutions nationwide. If your business is independently owned and operated, not dominant within its field, and falls within size standards, the SBA can be a useful resource. Each state has a US Small Business Administration (SBA) office and a Small Business Development Center (SBDC) network, cosponsored with the SBA and state-based college or university systems. These SBDCs employ professional counselors who provide guidance to small businesses at no charge. SCORE is another SBA-affiliated counseling network where business executives volunteer their time to assist smaller companies at no cost. Contact information for your local offices is listed in BUZGate.

Instructions: Call, then visit each of these organizations – build your network

SBA Office
Address
Telephone
Contact Person
e-Mail
Date of Contact
Result of Contact

SBDC Office	
Address	
Telephone	
Contact Person	
e-Mail	
Date of Contact	
Result of Contact	

SCORE Office	
Address	
Telephone	
Contact Person	
e-Mail	
Date of Contact	
Result of Contact	

8b. Banking Resource Networks

Banks are an essential part of any business operation. Even if you don't need to borrow money initially, you may need to do so as the business grows, and so relationships you can start today will help you in the future. There are a multitude of banking services any business needs, ranging from deposit (checking) accounts to merchant services (taking credit cards), to a whole range of other activities. The average commercial bank offers some 25 services of importance to small businesses. It is to your advantage to learn what they are and which will be valuable to you in your own business. Take the trouble to investigate more than one bank – some banks are much more small business friendly than others. Interview them to help decide who you would like to do business with – you are the customer and they want your business.

Instructions: Visit three or four banks to determine the one most suited to your business needs.

Bank Name:	
Address	
Telephone	
Contact Person	
e-Mail	
Date of Contact	
Result of Contact	

Bank Name:
Address
Telephone
Contact Person
e-Mail
Date of Contact
Result of Contact

Bank Name:
Address
Telephone
Contact Person
e-Mail
Date of Contact
Result of Contact

8c. Schools & Colleges Resource Networks

Academic institutions can be valuable resources for just about any type of business. Many schools offer business management training in credit or adult learning programs. Faculty members are expert in many different areas, and can often provide consultation for free or for a consulting fee. Most schools have a library that may be available to the public. Many schools have laboratory facilities that might be available as well. Often a business class may volunteer to work with a small business so that the students can gain real-world experience.

Instructions: Contact your local campus(es) to learn what might be available.

School Name:
Address
Telephone
Contact Person
e-Mail
Date of Contact
Result of Contact

School Name:
Address
Telephone
Contact Person
e-Mail
Date of Contact
Result of Contact

School Name:
Address
Telephone
Contact Person
e-Mail
Date of Contact
Result of Contact

8d. Professional Services Networks

Every business needs good accounting advice and, sooner or later, may need the services of an attorney as well. All businesses need insurance, whether it be liability, workers comp, fire and theft, health, and more. Often businesses can benefit from specialized consultants in areas such as marketing, production, or a range of other activities. Many of these professionals are listed in BUZGate in the Business-to-Business section (Go to www.BUZGate.org, click on your state, click on B2B). Other sources are to ask your banker or other professionals you also work with.

Instructions: Locate and interview each of the following professionals. Interview at least two of each. They should not charge for this exploratory interview.

Questions for an Accountant:
- o Do you work with small firms of (state your business type)?
- o What level of accounting and / or bookkeeping support do you provide?
- o Do you recommend and support Quick Books or some other automated accounting system?
- o Will you provide advice on a monthly basis?
- o How do you calculate your fees? What is your estimated monthly charge?

Accountant Name:
Address
Telephone
Contact Person
e-Mail
Date of Contact
Result of Contact

Accountant Name:
Address
Telephone
Contact Person
e-Mail
Date of Contact
Result of Contact

Questions for an Attorney:

- o Do you work with small firms of (state your business type)?
- o What level of service do you typically provide?
- o Will you provide advice on an as-needed basis?
- o How do you calculate your fees? What is your estimated monthly charge? Is there a retainer?

Attorney Name:
Address
Telephone
Contact Person
e-Mail
Date of Contact
Result of Contact

Attorney Name:
Address
Telephone
Contact Person
e-Mail
Date of Contact
Result of Contact

Questions for an Insurance Broker:

- o   Do you work with small firms of (state your business type)?
- o   What type of service do you typically provide – Comprehensive Business, Workers Comp, Health, other?
- o   Do you represent a single insurance company? Or do you shop different companies for the best rates
- o   How are premiums calculated and how are they paid?

Insurance Broker Name:
Address
Telephone
Contact Person
e-Mail
Date of Contact
Result of Contact

Insurance Broker Name:
Address
Telephone
Contact Person
e-Mail
Date of Contact
Result of Contact

8e. Business Incubator Resource Networks

Business incubators are places where emerging businesses can rent a small amount of space inexpensively and without a long-term lease. There are typically many other services available including shared office equipment and services, training, mentoring, and great networking.

Instructions: Determine if there is an incubator in your area by visiting www.nbia.org. If so, give them a call to find if this is a suitable resource for you.

Incubator Name:
Address
Telephone
Contact Person
e-Mail
Date of Contact
Result of Contact

8f. Additional Business Support Networks

There are a number of private sector resource providers that offer high value products and services. These are listed in the Business Utility Zone Gateway (www.BUZGate.org).

Accounting
Bankruptcy Alternative
Business Plan Template
Business Taxes Solutions
Cash Management
Debt Management
Expense Management
Inventory Management
Order Processing
Outsourcing Accounts Receivable
Receipt Management

Finance
Alternative Funding
Business Charge Card
Business Credit
Debt Restructuring
Factoring
Funding from Family

Sales and Marketing
Audio Conferencing
Conferencing Facilities
Customer Relations Marketing
eMail Marketing
eNewsletters
Internet Marketing Strategy
Marketing Communications
Online Store
Printing Services
Sales Templates
Search Engine Optimization (SEO)
Web Site Design
Web Site Development
Web Site Promotion

Facilities
Office Space On-Demand
Remote Conferencing

Insurance
Health Insurance

Management
Business Counseling Solutions
Business Startup
Disaster Recovery
Innovation Center
Supplier Communications

Human Resources
Employee Background Checks
Employee Communications
Employment Forms
Employee Manual Template
Health Insurance

IT and Communications
Conferencing Services
Ecommerce Software
eMail Marketing Software
Information Transfer Technologies
Remote Access
Web Conferencing

Administration
Business Document Templates
Business Productivity Software
Logistics Transportation
Order Fulfillment
Warehouse Storage

Productivity Enhancers
Document Management
Networked Copier, Printer & Fax
Online Surveys
Outsourced Receptionist
Scanner Software
Sales Proposal Templates
Consulting Proposals
General Sales Proposal
Marketing Proposals
Web Development Proposal

Travel
Global Office On-Demand
Virtual Office Program

Summary Step 8

The goal in this Step is to identify and develop the public and private resources you will need to build your business success.

Instructions: Fill in the data from your earlier work:

Resource Network			
Resource	**Contact Name**	**Phone**	**e-Mail**
US SBA			
SBDC			
SCORE			
Bank #1			
Bank #2			
Bank #3			
Academic Institution			
Accountant			
Attorney			
Insurance Broker			
Incubator			
Other			

Now on to Step 9....

9

STEP 9

Business Launch

Do I have the licenses, approvals and other issues covered that are needed for actually starting the new business?

In this Section:

- o   Introduction
- o   Start-Up Requirements
- o   Regulations and other Compliance Issues
- o   Managing Business Risk
- o   Strategic Mapping
- o   Exercises:
  - o   Business Readiness Checklist
  - o   Strategic Mapping Worksheet
  - o   Summary Step 9

Step 9

Business Launch

Introduction

All of the work you have done so far is to prepare for what you may have thought would be your first activity – opening for business. Even now, though, there is more information you may need to gather and other issues to prepare for before you are actually ready to "open the doors." The Business Readiness Checklist will help you to identify what these final issues may be.

Start-Up Requirements

Do you know what needs to be done to actually start your business??

Use the Business Readiness Checklist so that you do not miss something important!

There may be business licensing, zoning requirements, occupancy permits, or other state and local requirements that you will have to comply with. Don't forget about or ignore the need for risk prevention and insurance. Your business development resource provider, your lawyer, or accountant will help you with the specifics.

The point is, be prepared – otherwise you may be shut down even before you start.

Regulations and Other Compliance Issues

Depending on the nature of your business, there may be various permits and licenses you need to obtain before you can "open for business." These are not normally difficult to obtain. However, if you neglect to apply for them in time, they can become a serious hold-up to your operation.

The place to start is the town or city hall for the area where your business will be located. They will inform you of local regulations. You can check with your regional planning commission for other area regulations and requirements. The trade association for your type of business can inform you of state and regional requirements for your particular industry. The local SBDC office will normally have a list of regulations for different types of business. Your lawyer can be a final resource once you have pursued the no-cost avenues. Investigate these resources early in the development process so you won't unknowingly create a problem for yourself.

Labor laws and regulations ranging from minimum wage, employing juveniles, hours, sexual harassment and other issues can represent serious problems if not properly addressed. The local Department of Labor office can provide much valuable advice. A payroll service can be a valuable resource to help with many of these issues as well. Work place safety is governed by Occupational Safety and Health Administration (OSHA) rules and regulations, and other safety issues by Environmental Protection Administration (EPA) rules and regulations. Much valuable advice is available through their web sites and from their local/regional offices.

Find Free Help

Find public sector programs that can provide help and direction to you at no cost at:

www.BUZGate.org

The public sector programs are listed at www.BUZGate.org. Here you will find the listing for your local regional planning commission, various trade associations and local SBDC office.

The Secretary of State office for your state or Department of Economic Development may have a list of state and local regulations as well.

Managing Business Risk

Managing risk can be one of the most important things you do to maintain the viability of your business. You've probably heard the horror stories about lawsuits that arise from careless hiring practices or major property expenses that result from a simple repair job left undone. Too often, major losses could have been avoided by simple attention to prevention early on. Purchasing business insurance can be a wise choice in preparing for the unexpected. There are many different types and many different prices. Investigate providers, coverage and costs to determine what makes the most sense for you and your operation. Follows is a summary of different types of insurance coverage. This summary was prepared by the US Small Business Administration.

General Liability

Many business owners buy general liability or umbrella liability insurance to cover legal hassles due to claims of negligence. These help protect against payments as the result of bodily injury or property damage, medical expenses, the cost of defending lawsuits, and settlement bonds or judgments required during an appeal procedure.

Product Liability

Every product is capable of personal injury or property damage. Companies that manufacture, wholesale, distribute, and retail a product may be liable for its safety. Additionally, every service rendered may be capable of personal injury or property damage. Businesses are considered liable for negligence, breach of an express or implied warranty, defective products, and defective warnings or instructions.

Home-Based Business Insurance

Contrary to popular belief, homeowners' insurance policies do not generally cover home-based business losses. Commonly needed insurance areas for home-based businesses include business property, professional liability, personal and advertising injury, loss of business data, crime and theft and disability.

Internet Business Insurance

Web-based businesses may wish to look into specialized insurance that covers liability for damage done by hackers and viruses. In addition, e-insurance often covers specialized online activities, including lawsuits resulting from Meta tag abuse, banner advertising, or electronic copyright infringement.

Worker's Compensation

Required in every state except Texas, worker's compensation insurance pays for employees' medical expenses and missed wages if injured while working. The amount of insurance employers must carry, rate of payment, and what types of employees must be carried varies depending on the state. In most cases, business owners, independent contractors, domestic employees in private homes, farm workers, and unpaid volunteers are exempt.

Criminal Insurance

No matter how tight security is in your workplace, theft and malicious damage are always possibilities. While the dangers associated with hacking, vandalism, and general theft are obvious, employee embezzlement is more common than most business owners think. Criminal insurance and employee bonds can provide protection against losses in most criminal areas.

Business Interruption Insurance

It is possible to acquire insurance that covers losses during natural disasters, fires, and other catastrophes that may cause the operation to shut down for a significant amount of time.

Key Person Insurance

In addition to a business continuation plan that outlines how the company will maintain operations if a key person dies, falls ill, or leaves, some companies may wish to buy key person insurance. This type of coverage is usually life insurance that names the corporation as a beneficiary if an essential person dies or is disabled.

Malpractice Insurance

Some licensed professionals need protection against payments as the result of bodily injury or property damage, medical expenses, the cost of defending lawsuits, investigations and settlements, and bonds or judgments required during an appeal procedure.

Further information can be found at the SBA website: http://www.sba.gov/smallbusinessplanner/manage/getinsurance/SERV_INSURANCE.html

Exercises Step 9: Business Launch

9a. Business Readiness Checklist

9b: Strategic Mapping Worksheet

9c. Summary Step 9

Now on to the exercises....

9a: Business Readiness Check List

The Business Readiness Check List will help you identify the various issues you must be on top of, before you can actually start your new business.

Instructions: Carefully review the Business Readiness Check List to identify issues you need to plan for. Place an "X" by those already addressed, an "O" by those that do not apply, and a "?" by those that need further attention. Create an action plan for each identified with a question mark.

Business Readiness Check List			
Registrations And Regulations	**Status**		
1. Establish a business location	X	O	?
o Licenses, permits – Check with the local town or city hall regarding permit, zoning, and licensing requirements for your specific business and location			
o Lease or rent agreements – Read carefully before you sign any applicable agreements – seek legal advice where necessary			
2. Select a name for your business	X	O	?
o Business name – Choose a name that will be easy for customers to remember and that stands out from your competition			
o Register the name of your business with your Secretary of State's office			
o URL – Consider how your business name may translate into a name for your website			
3. Choose a business structure	X	O	?
o Review "Types of Business Entities" in BUZGate FAQ's to understand the types of business formations available for establishing your venture. For additional advice on which type to choose, consult with your accountant or attorney			
4. File for an Employer Identification number (EIN) with the IRS	X	O	?
o This must be completed if you plan on having employees work for you and is useful for a variety of other purposes. Visit "Obtaining a Tax ID" section in BUZGate FAQs for an EIN application			
5. Business Law	X	O	?
o Do you know which business laws you must obey?			
o Do you have a lawyer that can help you with your business law needs? Go to the American Bar Association and locate an appropriate lawyer in your area (http://www.abanet.org)			
Insurance	**Status**		
1. Determine your business insurance needs	X	O	?
o What insurance will you need to protect yourself and your business? Review the listing in the prior section			
o Work with a qualified professional and purchase an appropriate policy – do not hesitate to interview more than one provider – three is a good reference – You want someone you can trust and depend on to help you			

Business Readiness Check List (Continued)

Record Keeping	Status		
1. Plan a system for recording important financial information	X	O	?
o Seek the advice of an accountant or consultant to understand how to set up a bookkeeping system and provide for regular reports, filings, and review			
o Do not start your operation until you have a bookkeeping system in place!!			
2. Plan a system for recording and paying taxes	X	O	?
o Work with an accountant or consultant to determine what taxes you must pay and when – check the IRS website: http://www.irs.gov/businesses/small/article/0,,id=176080,00.html			
o If you plan to have employees, you will need a system for deducting taxes – consider a payroll service			
3. Plan a system for recording and tracking inventory levels	X	O	?
o Determine what level of inventory is needed to operate the business and use a tracking system			
4. Plan a system for planning, recording and tracking employees time			
o Set up a planning and tracking system to make sure that all important tasks are covered – Check BUZGate Free Tools for tracking tools			
Advertising	**Status**		
1. Advertise your business and location	X	O	?
o For physical locations choose a sign that is easily read by passing customers and attracts attention (make sure you check local sign ordinances)			
o Internet presence – for a web-based business (or any other), work with a professional to develop a functional website that serves your business purposes			
o Website visibility – Work with a professional to implement a website awareness campaign; search engine optimization, reciprocal link strategies (see the Web Marketing article in BUZGate)			
o Select and promote your opening date – plan how to advertise to your target market			
Utilities	**Status**		
1. Make arrangements for needed utilities	X	O	?
o If home-based, select telephone and Internet service that well support the business use – and is separate from your home use – Shop around!!			
o If operating out of a location other than your home, you will need to arrange for utilities (heat, electricity, phone, etc.)			
Equipment & Supplies	**Status**		
1. Decide and purchase necessary equipment, technology and supplies	X	O	?
o Determine what equipment, and related systems you will need, and choose a reliable vendor			
o Build a relationship for repeat orders and support			
o Choose your computer vendor carefully – you may well need set-up support and ongoing service, so make sure you are not just getting a great bargain – Also make sure that they have references and are reliable			

LAUNCH THE VENTURE!!!

Strategic Mapping

Now that you are getting ready for the launch, take some time to review the planning elements you have been assembling. They come together is a specific manner to create an integrated whole. You will look at this again at the end of Step 10, as the foundation stones for building your Knowledge Management System (*KMS*).

Strategic Mapping is a complete business management process comprised of interrelated and interdependent parts, integrated into a coherent action plan. It starts with defining strategic objectives, moves thorough a process of tactical evaluation, and results in a knowledge control system. Your control systems provide the information and feedback you need to monitor the progress of the plan and the business operation itself. This planning process is a way of defining what needs to be done today and tomorrow to achieve future goals. It is comprised of specific elements of work that are assigned to named individuals and monitored to show progress.

Strategic Mapping
How key elements fit together

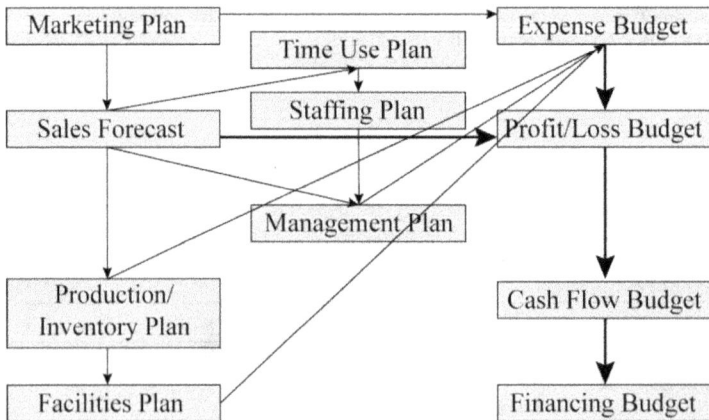

Strategic Mapping represents a rational approach to business development

- o It provides an understandable way to deal with complexity – without getting lost in the confusion

- o It allows us to build the business strategy piece by piece, yet ensures that the parts add up to the whole

- o It allows identification of, and developing an action plan for, each discrete element of the business process needed for success

- o It then supports the combining of these elements into a coherent whole – An integrated management system

- o It is a modular business development process that also represents a modular control system

Strategic Mapping

Integrating the parts to make the plan

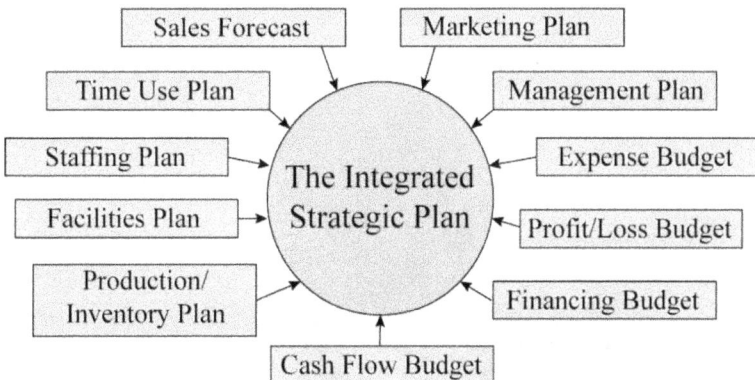

Sales Forecast · Marketing Plan · Time Use Plan · Management Plan · Staffing Plan · Expense Budget · Facilities Plan · The Integrated Strategic Plan · Profit/Loss Budget · Production/Inventory Plan · Financing Budget · Cash Flow Budget

9b. Strategic Mapping Worksheet

We provided you with the Strategic Mapping Worksheet in Step 6 (page 107). The worksheet is provided again in this step to allow you to revisit your ideas and make any changes necessary.

The Strategic Mapping Worksheet allows you to summarize your goals in a trackable format where the actions and decisions you make for today and tomorrow are in direct alignment with your longer term goals. This Worksheet brings about an alignment between the planning process and its implementation.

Instructions: Using the data you have compiled through the different exercises up to this Step, complete the worksheet, extending these projections into a three year time frame. Once you have completed the sheet here, go back and look at your answers in Step 6. You may well have changed your ideas of what is possible / feasible!

9b: Strategic Mapping Worksheet

STRATEGIC MAPPING WORKSHEET						
Projected & Actual Results	3 Year Goal	2 Year Goal	1 Year Goal	Present Year	Past Year	Past 2 Years
Sales						
Gross Margin						
Net Profit (EBIT)						
Breakeven						
Inventory						
Units Produced						
Units Sold						
Number of Customers						
Advertising Budget (% of Sales)						
Number of Employees						
Number of Locations						
Place a checkmark for the following where applicable						
Geographic Penetration						
Local						
Regional						
National						
International						
Internet Presence						
Website						
E-Commerce Site						
Other Factors						

Understand the Information Needs For Your Venture

Four Step Common Sense Knowledge Management System

1. Define business information needs

2. Build an information map

3. Turn information into Knowledge

4. Utilize and distribute knowledge answers

Summary Step 9

The goal in this Step is to identify issues such as regulations and related requirements that you need to address before you launch the venture.

Instructions: List the four most important issues your need to address, and your action items for each:

Business Launch Requirements	
Requirement	**Action**
1.	
2.	
3.	
4.	

Now on to Step 10....

Run Your Business....

Don't Let It Run You!!!

10

STEP 10

Monitor Progress

Am I prepared to monitor and control operations once started?

In this Section:

- o   Introduction
- o   Record Keeping and Management
- o   Knowledge Management Systems (KMS)
    - o   Define Business Information Needs
    - o   Build an Information Map
    - o   Turn Information Into Knowledge
    - o   Utilize and Distribute Knowledge Answers
- o   Counseling Resources
- o   Exercises:
    - o   Business Monitoring Strategy Worksheet
    - o   KMS Worksheet
    - o   Summary Step 10

Step 10

Monitor Progress

Introduction

All too often, people get so consumed with the day-to-day issues of running the business, that they forget about or do not allocate the time and resources for the bookkeeping, record keeping and other management tasks that are essential to making sure that their business operation is on track and that problems are not developing that they may be unaware of.

Start-up operations frequently ignore the need for these activities or plan to do the tasks themselves. Here is an area where hiring the right professional is not only smart, but can (and should) be a critical part of your management plan. If you have employees, a payroll service is a bargain. Surprisingly, the IRS is a valuable resource, not only laying out business tax responsibilities, but providing other helpful advice as well.

Record Keeping & Management

Your Business Plan is Your Plan of Action

Use it daily to stay on track with the events and actions that must be accomplished to achieve your longer term business success

In Step 5, we discussed the importance of developing a business plan. The real importance is that the business plan is really your plan of action. As such, it should be on your desk (and not in the closet or file drawer), and providing the day-to-day guidance you need in running the operation.

It is far too easy to become distracted by the day-to-day and even minute-to-minute demands on your time, and so loose track of the critical actions needed to achieve the success of your venture. Your business plan is your best plan of action – follow it!

The Business Utility Zone Gateway (www.BUZGate.org) contains a wealth of management information and related tools. You can read articles and download worksheets on a range of topics.

Free Business Articles	Free Business Forms
Avoiding Burnout	Breakeven Worksheet
Breakeven Analysis	Cash Flow Worksheet
Business Network Building	Communication Log
Business Planning	Functional Time Use Analysis
Business Plan Outline	Financing Chart
Cash Management	Organizational Mapping
Financing Proposal	Start-up Checklist
Management Control	Personal Financial Statement
No Cost Low Cost Marketing	Time Planning Schedule
Protect Business Assets	Web Marketing Checklist
Risk Management (PDF file)	
Succession Planning	
SWOT Analysis	
Web Marketing	

The US Small Business Administration (SBA) website provides links to a number of free publications that deal with a wide range of small business development and management issues. Follow the link below to the publications section.

The Internal Revenue Service (IRS) website provides valuable information about what records to help track and monitor the progress of your small business. To view a comprehensive article as well as links to record keeping examples when starting out, follow the link below. Read the information provided there and select additional links relative to your own perceived record keeping needs.
http://www.irs.gov/businesses/small/article/0,,id=98551,00.html

Exercises Step 10: Monitor Progress

10a. Business Monitoring Strategy Worksheet

10b: KMS Worksheet

10c. Summary Step 10

Now on to the exercises....

10a: Business Monitoring Strategy Worksheet

Instructions: Describe your management strategy for each of the issues listed

Business Monitoring Strategy Worksheet
1. Financial Management Strategy
Accounting System Plan
Monthly / Quarterly Budget Deviation Analysis Plan
Banking / Money Management Plan
Financial Advisor / CFO Plan
2. Human Relations Management Strategy
Employment Requirements Plan
Payroll Management Plan
Labor Regulations Compliance Plan

Business Monitoring Strategy Worksheet (Continued)

3. Sales / Customer Development Strategy
Sales Plan
Marketing Plan
Customer Management And Record Keeping Plan

4. Strategic Planning Strategy
Business Plan Monitoring
Business Plan Updating

5. Resource Network Strategy
Resource Network Maintenance Plan

6. Risk Management Strategy
Insurance Plan
Labor Law Compliance Plan
OSHA / EPA Compliance Plan

Knowledge Management Systems (KMS)

Turning people, process and technology into knowledge

Why Knowledge Management?

Knowledge management is a process of organizing and integrating the sources and flows of information within your business so that they result in answers. Knowledge systems reduce the complexity of running a business by implementing decision rules where appropriate and monitoring the results through a process of deviation analysis. Knowledge management is the bridge between business management needs and information technology capabilities. It is business intelligence data transformed into rational business management systems. Our Knowledge Management System (*KMS*) is a business intelligence system that will allow you to control your operation, rather than have it control you. Good goals.

1. Define Business Information Needs

The answers to the following questions provide the foundation stones of the *KMS*: *What do you need to know? Why do you need to know it?*

The first stage in the planning process is preparing a list of objectives. These objectives provide the groundwork for establishing the balance of the strategy framework and lend a sense of both consistency and perspective to the other planning and business development activities. Together, these goals are essential to the coordination and integration of all subordinate-planning activities. They help to ensure that each of the different areas of organizational activities are complementary and not at odds with each other.

The key function of the strategic plan is to provide guidelines for day-to-day decision making. Specific activities relate to tasks that relate to goals. Once goals, objectives, and the delegation of responsibility and authority have been made explicit, control benchmarks can be established. These benchmarks are then used to monitor the progress of the business. Goals become the targets or points of reference for measuring progress. When such guidelines are available, deviations can be identified and evaluated quickly and the causes for deviations, both positive and negative, can be determined. Potential problems are revealed and opportunities identified.

The most serious problem we find people encountering in the business development process is the difficulty of being specific about what they want to accomplish. Vague generalities such as, "We want to be successful," certainly express a real concern. Most businesses want to be successful. There are much more important aspects to the question though: Successful at what? In what way? How is success to be measured? How will you know when you have gotten there? Be specific.

Objectivity in the goal setting process is essential to managing the *KMS* activities. Typically, objective goals can be quantified. Once quantified, actual performance can be compared against that planned (budgeted), and differences expressed as deviations. The *KMS* takes each of these planning activities and the resulting units of work and responsibility, and provides the framework to aid in assembling the various pieces into a coherent whole package.

2. Build an Information Map

Identify and locate needed information: *Where is the data/information? How will you get it?*

Once you have defined what information you will need, the process of building an information map is quite straightforward. Once goals are established, results are compared to expectations to determine how well the operation is doing. As you begin to visualize this process for your own operation, the flows of feedback information, such as deviation reports, needed to tell you "how well you are doing" will start to become obvious. As these reporting requirements emerge, they allow you to also identify where the supporting information must come from.

The planning tools and systems each defines a flow of information - primarily through the accounting system, although some will come from other, slightly softer systems, such as employee evaluations, where the work reviewed is compared against the goals previously set, and deviations from these goals are noted. Building the

Information Map is a matter of listing each of the sub-planning systems, identifying what information is needed, identifying where it is within (or even outside of) the company, and how it gets to where it is needed and/or to whom needs to use it. The worksheet at the end of this article will help you to build this information map for your own operation.

3. Turn Information into Knowledge

Information/Data: H*ow will you use it? What does it mean? What is it trying to tell you?*

Managing with a knowledge system is not magic, complicated, impossible to understand, or even difficult – it is instead very straightforward. Once you begin to use these tools, you will quickly gain confidence and competence in this new style of management.

The knowledge management rule of information is: Process + Context = Relevance. Knowledge is the result of adding utility to information/data. Information reduction (process) and information meaning (context) are the two activities that transform the information overload into something useful.

Information Reduction requires limiting in some manner, the amount of information or data we actually look at. The goal is to establish information decision rules that screen out data that does not have to be personally inspected. With this qualifying approach, it is then necessary only to know that these desired activities actually occurred. Feedback systems (deviation analysis) will tell us this.

Information Meaning provides an appropriate context. Is something too big, too little, too hot, etc.? These qualities have meaning only when compared against something else. It is not enough to tell employees that they need to work harder. How much harder? How will both management and the employees know that the employees are meeting company expectations? The data regarding performance needs to be very precise. Determining how many units they presently make per hour is very straightforward – we count them in some manner. The essential context is how many units are expected. For non-manufacturing operations projects are mutually defined and results and completion dates agreed to. These become the performance evaluation criteria. Once this context is established, employees can know exactly how much (or if at all) they must improve their performance. Management only needs to know when the goal is not achieved. A deviation report will provide the needed information.

The most common knowledge system is a monthly budget deviation report. A great deal of time and trouble goes into establishing budgets that are related to key aspects critical to the operation such as sales revenues, cash flows, variable costs, and fixed expenses. It is necessary to know when each of these are under or over budget as quickly as possible. With the accounting tools commonly available today, this data can be captured in real time – actually minute by minute as it is generated and recorded within the company. This information can then be displayed on a computer as a "dashboard," showing these critical parameters and whether each are within or out of spec. Where out of spec, it is possible to click on that parameter, and drill down into the associated databases to the extent of detail required to determine the cause for the deviation and form a course of action to bring it back into line with the plan.

Knowledge/deviation/dashboard systems can report on practically all activities of any business. Processing this data through information reduction (to get to the heart of the matter), and giving it context (relational meaning), provides the tools needed to effectively manage any operation.

4. Utilize and Distribute Knowledge Answers

Knowledge: *How will you share it?*

Planning systems are used to create management imperatives. Knowledge systems are then used to generate and get the right information/knowledge answers to the right individuals within the company. With this essential information, employees can effectively perform the work required for the company's success.

Summary

Our *KMS* is a business intelligence system that will allow you to productively address key business questions, and to control your operation, rather than have it control you. The *KMS* provides a total framework to aid in assembling the various strategic components into a coherent whole management package, along with the information flows required to make sure that the operation stays on track. The *KMS* will help to ensure that the critical information needed to run your business successfully is in the context you need, when you need it, and that it flows to the necessary personnel within the organization. Balancing control and flexibility - what does it all mean? Make more money in your business and enjoy it more.

10b: Knowledge Management Systems (*KMS*) Worksheet

The Knowledge Management Systems (KMS) worksheet is a way to identify and systematically organize all of the essential flows of information within the business so that intelligent use can be made of the data collected. You have gone to the trouble of establishing budgets for these different categories. Now, the budgets become the basis for your deviation reports. A deviation report is simply a way to compare the actual performance with the planned, forecast performance, and looking at differences, if any. Differences then are the trigger to review that aspect of your operation and see what needs to be done to bring reality into line with the expectation.

Instructions: Look at each of the sub-planning categories listed on the left side of the Worksheet as a data source for your KMS. Think about how you can organize the flows of data and information within your business so that you can create your own *KMS*.

10b: Knowledge Management Systems (*KMS*) Worksheet

Strategic Planning Category	Measurement Criteria	Source of Data	Evaluation Criteria	Required Action
P&L Plan (Budget)	Target Costs / Revenues, Target Ratios	Accounting System	Deviations from Benchmarks	
Cash Flow Plan	Target Revenues, Target Expenses	Accounting System	Deviations from Budget Categories	
Organizational Mapping	Functional Time Use Analysis	Human Resources	Task Sheet Logs Maintained / Reviewed	
Time / Use Budget	Employee Work Performance	Weekly Work Plan	Deviations from Project Target Deadlines	
Financing Plan	Achievement of Target Goals	Accounting System	Strategic Analysis	
Inventory Plan	Adequacy of Inventory	Inventory Control System	Stock-outs / Cost Budget	
Advertising / Marketing Plan	Sales Volume, Growth	Accounting System	Deviations from Forecast	
AR / AP Forecast	Age of A/R Age of A/P	Accounting System	Deviations from Forecast	
Development Plan	Meeting Time Goals	Various	PERT / CPM Other Tracking Systems	
Other				

About The Bonus Material

Make sure that you take a look at the Bonus Material that follows the Glossary. There are some very important tools that will aid you in your planning, evaluation and operation of your new venture. The planning and evaluation process never stops. That is the point of the Knowledge Management System.

Using the Problem Solving Approach will aid you in looking at any situation where you need to make a decision.

The Tactical Evaluation Process is a systematic way to look at every aspect of your business operation. It is a critical format for an annual review.

SWOT Analysis is one of the best ways to engage your employees and others who have an interest in your operation. It is another systematic process to identify the Strengths and Weaknesses of your business along with the Opportunities and Threats from the outside environment.

The Eupsychian Systems Approach helps you to understand what may be possible in a world that looks like it has so many barriers and constraints that you feel out of control.

Control is a good thing, and the more you are confident in using these and other tools to manage your operation, the greater your chances of success.

Summary Step 10

The goal in this Step is to identify issues such as regulations and related requirements that you need to address before you launch the venture.

Instructions: List the four most important issues your need to address, and your action items for each:

Business Monitoring Strategy	
Requirement	**Action**
1.	
2.	
3.	
4.	

Congratulations

You have completed the program and are now ready to move forward with the launch of your venture

Good Luck!!!

Glossary
of
Business Management Terms

Glossary of Business Management Terms

"Acid Test" Ratio

Cash plus those other assets that can be immediately converted to cash should equal or exceed current liabilities. The formula used to determine the ratio is as follows: cash plus receivables (net) plus marketable securities, divided by current liabilities. The "acid test" ratio is one of the most important credit barometers used by lending institutions, as it indicates the ability of a business enterprise to meet its current obligations.

Aging Receivables

A scheduling of accounts receivable according to the length of time they have been outstanding. This shows which accounts are not being paid in a timely manner and may reveal any difficulty in collecting long-overdue receivables. This may also be an important indicator of developing cash-flow problems.

Amortization

Liquidation on an installment basis; the process of gradually paying off a liability over a period of time (that is, a mortgage is amortized by periodically paying off part of the face amount of the mortgage).

Assets

The tangible resources, properties and property rights owned by an individual or business enterprise

Balance Sheet

An itemized statement that lists the total assets and the total liabilities of a given business to portray its net worth at a given moment in time

Breakeven Analysis

A method used to determine the point at which the business will neither make a profit nor incur a loss. That point is expressed in either the total dollars of revenue exactly offset by total expenses (fixed and variable); or in total units of production, the cost of which exactly equals the income derived by their sale.

Capital
> Capital funds are those funds that are needed for the base of the business. Usually they are put into the business in a fairly permanent form such as in fixed assets, plant and equipment, or they are used in other ways which are not recoverable in the short run unless you sell the entire business.

Capital Equipment
> Equipment that is used to manufacture a product, provide a service, or use to sell, store and deliver merchandise. Such equipment will not be sold in the normal course of business, but will be used and worn out or be consumed over time through the operation of the business.

Cash Flow
> The actual movement of cash within a business: cash inflow minus cash outflow. A term used to designate the reported net income of a corporation plus amounts charged off for depreciation, depletion, amortization, and extraordinary charges to reserves, which are bookkeeping deductions and not actually paid out in cash. Offers a better indication of the ability of a firm to meet its own obligations and to pay dividends than with the conventional net income figure

Cash Position
> See Liquidity

Construction Loans
> These loans are like a line of credit crossed with a term loan: as construction of, say, a building, reaches certain stages, the bank disburses money that is repayable over a lengthy period of time, usually in a flat monthly payment, through sometimes in a balloon payment that must be refinanced.

Corporation
> An artificial legal entity created by government grant and endowed with certain powers; a voluntary organization of persons, either actual individuals or legal entities, legally bound together to form a business enterprise.

Credit

Credit generally means trade credit unless stated otherwise, the accounts payable which suppliers and others may be willing to extend to a business. The credit terms are usually stated on the invoice as payment due within so many days, perhaps with a discount (reduced cost) available for early payment, and with added costs for paying later than the due date on the invoice. Trade credit is one of the major sources of financing for small businesses, and, for a stable small business, may be the major form of outside financing.

Current Assets

Cash or other items that will normally be turned into cash within one year and assets that will be used up in the operations of a firm within one year.

Current Liabilities

Amounts owed that will ordinarily be paid by a firm within one year. Such items include accounts payable, wages payable, taxes payable, the current portion of a long-term debt, and interest and dividends payable.

Current Ratio

Ratio of a firm's current assets to its current liabilities – the current ratio includes the value of inventories that have not yet been sold, so it is not the best evaluation of the current status of the firm. The "acid test" ratio, covering the most liquid of current assets, provides a better evaluation.

Deal

Refers to a proposal for financing business creation or expansion; a series of transactions and preparation of documents in order to obtain funds for business expansion or creation.

Debt

Debt refers to borrowed funds, whether from an individual's personal resources or from other individuals, banks, or other institutions. It is generally secured with a note, which in turn may be secured by a lien against property or other assets. Ordinarily, the note states repayment and interest provisions. These factors may vary greatly in both amount and duration depending upon the purpose, source and terms of the loan. Some debt is convertible; that is, it may be changed into direct ownership of a portion of a business under certain stated conditions.

Depreciation

A reduction in the value of fixed assets – the most important causes of depreciation are wear and tear, the effect of the elements, and gradual obsolescence that makes it unprofitable to continue using some assets until they have been exhausted. The purpose of the bookkeeping charge for depreciation is to write off the original cost of an asset (less expected salvage value) by equitably distributing charges against operations over the entire useful life of the asset.

Entrepreneur

Entrepreneur refers to an innovator of a business enterprise who recognizes opportunities to introduce a new product, a new production process, or an improved organization. An entrepreneur raises the necessary money, assembles the factors of production, organizes an operation to exploit the opportunity, and accepts the risk of potential failure of the venture.

Equity

Equity or net worth is the owner's investment in the business. Unlike capital, equity is what remains after the liabilities of the company are subtracted from the assets. Thus it may be greater than or less the capital invested in the business. Equity investment carries with it a share of ownership and usually a share in profits, as well as some say in how the business is managed. If you seek financing from outside investors, you may well find that the cost is parting with some equity; this sometimes is viewed as a threat to ownership even though effective control usually remains in the hands of the owner/manager.

Illiquid

See Liquidity

Limited Liability Company (LLC)

A limited liability company is a relatively new state-registered form of a business enterprise. For federal income tax purposes, it can be taxed as a proprietorship or partnership, but its members, like corporate shareholders, are not personally liable for the entity's debts and liabilities. Unlike a sub-chapter S corporation, there is no limit to the number of owners and different types of shareholders an LLC company may have.

Line of Credit

A source of funding that is either secured or unsecured; an agreement that ordinarily is renewed on an annual basis where a bank holds funds available for the use of a business. Usually an unsecured line will have to be completely paid out once a year. The advantage of a line of credit is that the money is there, ready to be used when needed, yet not costing more than a small fee until it is actually drawn upon. A credit card is a line of credit; it allows the individual to borrow up to a certain limit and make repayment in a pre-agreed fashion. No separate credit application is made at each use of the line. A line of credit is usually paid from normal operations; inventory is often seasonally financed under a line of credit, for example.

Liquidity

A term used to describe the solvency of a business, which has special reference to the degree of readiness in which assets can be converted into cash without a loss – also called cash position. If a firm's current assets cannot be converted into cash to meet current liabilities, the firm is said to be illiquid.

Loan Agreement

A loan agreement is a document that states repayment terms, interest rates, and usually, what a business can or cannot do as long as it owes money to (usually) a bank. A loan agreement may place restrictions on owner's salary, on dividends, on amount of other debt, on working capital levels, on sales, on number of added personnel, or whatever the lender views as a means of protection for the investment. It is helpful to note that while equity ordinarily controls a company, a loan agreement ensures that a large degree of control passes into the hands of the lender. This kind of agreement is frequently a condition of making a loan.

Loan

Debt money for small business is usually in the form of bank loans, loans that in a real sense are personal loans because a new small business is hard to evaluate in terms of creditworthiness and degree of risk, the two decisive variables in any judgment of making or not making a loan. A secured loan is a loan that is backed up by a claim against some asset or assets of a business; an unsecured loan is backed up by the faith the bank has in the borrower's ability to pay the money back. All loans fall into one of these categories. Note: The amount of collateral (assets securing the loan) asked for should always be considered – too much collateralization will restrict operational flexibility in the future. The purpose of collateral, incidentally, is to tie the individual to the deal, to make it hard to walk away if things get rough. Banks have no desire to become second-hand business-collateral dealers and even less desire to pull the personal assets of cosigners or co-makers. (Many bankers don't know this. They think, erroneously, that by securing the note with collateral they are making the loan "safer." They aren't.)

Long-Term Liabilities

Liabilities (expenses) that will not mature within the next twelve months

Market

The number of people and their total spending (actual or potential) for a product line or service within the geographic limits of the businesses' distribution capacity; market share is the percentage of the companies' sales compared to the sales of its competitors in total for a particular product or service

Note

The basic business loan – a note, represents a loan that will be repaid or substantially reduced thirty, sixty, or ninety days later at a stated interest rate. These are short-term, and unless they are made under a line of credit, a separate loan application is needed for each loan and each renewal.

Net Worth

> The owner's equity in a given business represented by the excess of the total assets over the total amounts owing to outside creditors (total liabilities) at a given moment in time. Also, the net worth of an individual as determined by deduction the amount of all his or her personal liabilities from the total value of his or her personal assets.

Partnership

> A legal relationship created by the voluntary association of two or more persons to carry on as co-owners of a business for profit; a type of business organization in which two or more persons agree on the amount of their contributions (capital and effort) and on the distribution of profits, if any.

Pro Forma

> The Proforma is a projection or estimate of what may result in the future from actions in the present. A pro forma financial statement is one that shows how the actual operations of the business will turn out if certain assumptions are realized.

Profit

> Profit is the excess of the selling price over all costs and expenses incurred in making the sale. Also, the reward to the entrepreneur for the risks assumed in the establishment, operation, and management of a given enterprise or undertaking.

Revolving Line of Credit

> Similar to a line of credit, except it does not normally need to be paid out annually. This kind of loan is of particular interest to a rapidly growing company with weak capitalization and may be converted to a term loan under certain conditions. But its basic purpose is the same as a line of credit

Sole Proprietorship or Proprietorship

> Refers to a type of business organization in which one individual owns the business. Legally, the owner is the business and personal assets are typically exposed to liabilities of the business.

Sub-Chapter S Corporation or Tax Option Corporation

> A corporation that has selected under Sub-chapter S of the IRS Tax Code (by unanimous consent of its shareholders) not to pay any corporate tax on its income and, instead, to have the shareholders pay taxes on it, even though it may or may not be distributed. Shareholders of a tax option corporation are also entitled to deduct, on their individual returns, their shares of any net operating loss sustained by the corporation, subject to limitations in the tax code. In many respects, Sub-chapter S permits a corporation to behave for tax purposes, as a proprietorship or partnership.

Subordinated Debt

> Subordinated debt is sometimes referred to as quasi-capital because it serves the same purposes as capital as far as a bank is concerned. Subordinating debt means placing that particular debt behind bank debt; that is, should the business fail and have to be sold for asset value, the bank gets paid before the holder of the subordinated debt. Often, the owners of a business will put loans made by them to the company in such a position which means that until the bank debt is paid off or reduced to a previously agreed amount, the owners cannot repay themselves.

Takeover

> Takeover refers to the acquisition of one company by another company.

Target Market

> The specific individuals, distinguished by socioeconomic, demographic, and/or interest characteristics, who are the most likely potential customers for the goods and/or services of a business.

Term Loan

> Either secured or unsecured, usually for periods of more than a year to as many as twenty years; term loans are paid off like a mortgage; so many dollars per month for so many years. The most common uses of term loans are for equipment and other fixed asset purposes, for working capital, and for real estate. Ordinarily, businesses do not

borrow for a year or less on a term basis; the cost to the bank would be excessive.

Working Capital

Working capital is the difference between current assets and current liabilities. Contrasted with capital, a permanent use of funds, working capital is for relatively short-term use. Working capital cycles through the business in a variety of forms: inventories, accounts and notes receivable, cash and securities, and prepaid expenses are but a few. Working capital shifts forms but remains an investment in and use of cash. Working capital may fluctuate in terms of seasonal needs. If a business has an inventory buildup prior to Christmas sales or the fall merchandising season, then the cash portion of working capital will be reduced; as the business sells off the inventory and retires payables, cash will increase. Due to this seasonal quality of working capital in some industries, it is wrong to rely too heavily on trade averages unless you know what point in the working capital cycle they come from.

Bonus Material

Contents

- o Five Steps to Effective Problem Solving
- o Eupsychian Systems Analysis (ESA)
- o Tactical Evaluation Process Worksheet
- o Using SWOT to Improve Your Business
- o SWOT Analysis Worksheet
- o Strategic Mapping Worksheet
- o Information Mapping Worksheet

Five Steps to Effective Problem Solving
Dr. William R. Osgood

As with most things, there is a methodical way to proceed with your business analysis. The following process will help you proceed through the business development and launch process.

Step 1: Identify Problem(s)

In looking at any business situation, identify as many problems (constraints) as possible. This takes us back to our listing of fixed and variable constraints introduced in ESA Goal Optimization (Step 2). Once identified, arrange the perceived problems in order of importance. The obvious problems are not necessarily the most important. Avoid value judgments and "villain" finding. Problems are not good or bad, they are simply limiting circumstances needing solutions. Put these ideas down on paper. Often, the process of writing them down forces you to clarify your thinking and may even put you closer in touch with reality.

Step 2: Identify Alternative Solutions

As you look for solutions, do not be bound by "obvious" answers. Use your imagination again. Consider all possible alternatives, even if some seem unlikely or even foolish. At this stage, do not worry about what might actually work. Thinking 'outside of the box' may actually lead you to solutions that would otherwise never have occurred to you. As well, always consider the 'do nothing' alternative. When you explore the consequences of inaction by default (or analysis paralysis), you may conclude that the 'do nothing' option is actually unacceptable, and that doing almost anything else is better.

Step 3: List the Consequences (Pros & Cons) of Each Alternative

Think through each of the alternative solutions you have listed. Define the strong and weak points of each. Be as clear as possible. Here it is important to set your biases aside, and try to think objectively. You are not finding the answer in this step; you are instead looking at the factors that will enable you to make the best choices.

Step 4: Select the "Best" Alternative

You have identified the possible choices and evaluated the pros and cons of each. If you have been careful in these earlier steps, your selection of the 'best' answer should be obvious. Obvious though it might be, still rationalize or defend your choice. Again, put your arguments on paper as though you were presenting the case to others. Indeed, you may be. But even if you are doing this for your own benefit the more formal process of committing these words to paper forces you to be more precise with your answers. It is important to note here that different individuals see different solutions. The only correct answer is the one you make work.

Step 5: Solution Implementation Plan

No strategy is complete without an action plan. Define clearly who is doing what, why, and how you will know when and how well it is done.

Eupsychian Systems Analysis (ESA)

Dr. William R. Osgood

ESA Goal Optimization – Five Steps

Eupsychian Systems Analysis (ESA) is a process of optimized goal setting. How can you know if your business is doing as well as possible? For most businesses, goal setting consists of defining targets relative to where the business has been: "We want to do 15% better than last year." What kind of a goal is this anyway? How do we know that last years level of activity was actually OK? How do we know that 15% more this year is OK – or even possible? This kind of marginal goal setting is generally an ineffective process and one that is almost guaranteed to be suboptimal. The dilemma is even worse for a new business. How do you even remotely know what may be possible?

ESA helps to define the most optimal targets. It provides a framework useful in modifying idealized, optimized goals within the reality of a given environment. Once goals are made both optimal and realistic, they become achievable. ESA is designed for problem solving involving multidimensional and interdependent subsystems in any setting, and is especially appropriate for use where the issues may not be so clear cut or obvious.

> **THE FIVE STEP EUPSYCHIAN SYSTEMS APPROACH TO GOAL SETTING**
> 1. Define the most ideal goal possible under utopian conditions
> 2. Identify real-world fixed and variable constraints
> 3. Modify the utopian goal relative to fixed constraints – bridge the gap between abstraction and reality
> 4. Establish change strategies to relax the variable constraints
> 5. Take action to achieve the now realistic composite goal

Step 1: Define the Most Ideal Goal Possible Under Utopian Conditions

This may sound too idealistic or even foolish at first – but how can we know how we are doing unless we know what is possible?

People often ask: "What is the limit on the size my business can grow to?" The right answer is – no limit – except the limitations caused by your own imagination and your fear of success. The limits of your imagination are caused by 'thinking in the box' – by being bound by the conventional, by the 'what is.' There is nothing necessarily wrong with this type of thinking except that it is inherently limiting. Instead, try thinking about 'what can be.' How do you 'think out of the box?' Why not think nationally – or even globally? So much is possible these days due to breakthroughs in technology and through such tools as the Internet. Why not have a chain of stores? How about international distribution of your manufactured products? Clearly, there are some limits – but we don't consider them until the next step! For now, we must let our imagination loose to the fullest.

What about the 'fear of success?' This is a very bothersome issue. What are you afraid of? People often respond to growth suggestions with: "We'd better be careful – we don't want to succeed too much!" Generally, this seems like crazy thinking. Understand what your fears are: losing control, working too hard, changing your management style, opening new facilities, raising money, and a whole list of possible issues. Write down these fears and examine them one by one. Developing your business growth strategy will be based on finding the answers to these potential problems. Keep in mind that there is nothing wrong with a desire to keep your business small. Just keep in mind as well though, that this <u>must</u> be your choice, and not the result of any set of outside factors. Once you have explicitly made this, or any other choice, you have accepted the responsibility for the future of your company. Only when you have done so can you begin to develop the strategy we discuss in the rest of this section.

Step 2: Identify Real-World Fixed and Variable Constraints

Analyze the actual situation to identify the fixed and variable factors that may inhibit reaching the utopian goal. This step is actually one of the most difficult parts of the process, and yet the most critical to the development of effective business change strategies. Here we inspect the reality of the environment our business operates within to identify the fixed and variable factors which may be goal limiting. There are certainly factors that may limit our ability to 'take over the world.' We may have already begun to identify some of these factors in our list of 'fears' we started in Step 1. We need to continue this listing as extensively as possible. It is important to list everything at first, even if some issues seem foolish or outrageous. When we have made the list, we can begin classification of these intervening factors as fixed or variable. Fixed factors are those we have no control over. They may include the state of the economy, laws and regulations, competition, or other such external factors. Variable factors are more controllable issues such as whether we can hire a particular needed talent we do not presently employ, or can somehow raise the funds we do not presently have access to. The fixed factors are absolute constraints on what we can achieve. The variable factors have solutions, although the solutions may not be immediately apparent.

Step 3:   Modify the Utopian Goal Relative to Fixed Constraints – Bridge the Gap between Abstraction and Reality

Once we have made our list of factors and separated it into the two categories of fixed and variable, we can proceed with defining our business development strategies. We first return to Step 1 and modify our utopian vision by the reality constraints we have identified as fixed (can't be changed) factors. Now we know what is at least theoretically possible. Usually this is a very big surprise. Typically what is shown to be possible through this process is much greater than what we thought in our wildest dreams. This is good news for those who truly want to grow their businesses to the greatest level possible. For those who desire a smaller scale operation, this is still valuable information as they can now create their plan based on a 'big picture' view.

Step 4:   Establish Change Strategies to Relax the Variable Constraints

Variable factors are, by definition, changeable. We have some degree of control over these issues. Sometimes that control is much greater than we originally believed possible. By going through a process of free thinking once again (as in Step 1), we may find some very creative ways to overcome obstacles that we previously accepted as limiting facts of life. For example, if it is more financing that we require, let's explore all options. It is frequently possible to have suppliers extend longer credit terms, or we may be able to get our customers to pay more quickly, thus reducing the working capital we might otherwise need to develop through other sources. We can also consider exploring lease versus purchase alternatives. Factoring accounts receivable is another source that is typically not well utilized by smaller companies. There is a considerable network of "angel investors." Some of these examples are areas where outside help can prove valuable. Explore what the U.S. Small Business Administration (SBA) may have available for help, along with SCORE, your local Small Business Development Center (SBDC), the state department of economic development, and a great many other such resources commonly available in your local community.

Each of the other variable factors may well have a similar range of relief options when you once again, step 'out of the box,' and open your mind to what may be possible.

Step 5: Take Action to Achieve the Now Realistic Composite Goal

Now you are finally in a position to proceed with creating a realistic strategic vision and a practical plan that is likely to work. Goals become strategy, strategy becomes action plans and action plans become someone's work plan. Until this occurs, nothing will happen. In fact, and as we will repeat many times, planning without action is a waste of time. Use this advice to build an action plan to achieve the results you now know are possible. Through a delta (or gap) analysis, we can now compare where we are with where we want to be. Where we want to be minus where we are equals what needs to be done. Strategic analysis is nothing more than carefully thinking though all of the options.

Tactical Evaluation Process

Dr. William R. Osgood

1. Identify what the company is now

   a. Background History
      o Senior management perspective: General description of what the company is today – culture, mission, personalities, stories
      o General company history and structure
      o List 2-3 seminal events that caused / will cause the company to change (acquisition, new products)
      o Operations and marketing history: Show graphically (time, %, numbers)
      o Attitudes towards risk: How aggressive is the company in achieving its goals – risk-averse, moderate, or aggressive? Rank the company on an aggressiveness scale of 1 – 10, with 1 being the least aggressive
      o Attitude towards Investment: Risk translates into investment – more aggressive will take bolder plans

   b. Internal Drivers: Standardize the company value system
      o Which group internally is dominant: production, product development, marketing, financial? What is important to each of the subgroups? What do they think of each other? Make a matrix
      o What is the attitude toward the customer?

   c. Internal Strengths/Weaknesses of the company – These factors identify or describe the capacity and resources or lack thereof within the business
      o List 10 for each and then prioritize in terms of importance. Have each key participant make a list independently of the others, then consolidate the lists, and discuss – give everyone an opportunity to argue, then vote to reach a consensus

   d. External Opportunities & Threats facing the business – These factors identify factors that will support or inhibit company activities

- o Identify 5 trends affecting society as a whole : economic, social & political
- o Identify 5 trends affecting the industry that the company serves
- o Identify 5 trends directly affecting the business
- o Integrate these three lists, and prioritize by order of importance to the company. These trends identify and describe the environment within which the business operates.

e. Analytic empirical information about the company (this is factual data, not opinions)

- o Use as spreadsheet to show your P&L data by quarter for the past 3 years – what are the trends in sales, expenses, other trends?
- o Hierarchical company ranking for your SIC code will show you where you stand relative to others
- o What does it cost you to acquire a customer vs. the industry average?
- o Define your customer relative to Recency, Frequency, and Monetary Value
- o What is your cost to retain a customer?
- o List your top 10 (100) (1,000) customers by sales and/or profitability
- o Apply the 80/20 rule to your customers.

USING SWOT ANALYSIS TO IMPROVE YOUR BUSINESS
Dr. William R. Osgood

A key problem facing any smaller business is how to focus their limited business resources of time and money. SWOT analysis provides an efficient way to evaluate the range of factors that influence any operation, and can provide valuable guidance in making decisions about what to do next. It also provides a highly productive way to get key personnel involved in the management decision-making process.

SWOT analysis the process of carefully inspecting the business and its environment through the various dimensions of Strengths, Weaknesses, Opportunities, and Threats. Strengths are the company's core competencies, and include proprietary technology, skills, resources, market position, patents, and others. Weaknesses are conditions within the company that can lead to poor performance, and can include obsolete equipment, no clear strategy, heavy debt burden, poor product or market image, weak management, and others. Opportunities are outside conditions or circumstances that the company could turn to its advantage, and could include a specialty niche skill or technology that suddenly realizes a growth in broad market interest. Threats are current or future conditions in the outside environment that may harm the company, and might include population shifts, changes in purchasing preferences, new technologies, changes in governmental or environmental regulations, or an increase in competition.

As with most such management analysis tools, SWOT in of itself will not give specific answers. Instead, it is a way to organize information and assign probabilities to potential events - both good and bad - as the basis for developing business strategy and operational plans.

Using SWOT analysis is a straightforward process. The key is to limit the number of issues under each category. This process forces you to evaluate the relative importance of each, and select only the most critical; to get there, use a reduction process.

List any issues you can think of that affect your business. These may be extremely pragmatic and objective (we don't have enough capital to support growth), or highly subjective (key personnel don't like each other and so don't work well together). They may be internal or external. They may be real or perceived. Don't evaluate at this stage; just make your list.

Once listed, sort these issues or factors into the SWOT categories.

Sort each category first by relative importance, and then by reality. This is where the hard work begins. It is critical at this stage to make sure that the factors you are listing are real and not wistful thinking on your part (We are the best - Are you really the best? How? Why?), or a way of passing the buck (Things are out of control, and there is nothing I can do about it). Being honest with yourself here is essential.

Now, use the reduction process to limit each list to no more than five factors or issues. This forces you to look for duplicates or variations of the same issue, and to determine which are really the most critical to your business situation.

Once you have performed the SWOT analysis yourself, ask your key employees to go through the same process. Make sure that they do this independently of your work and each other, otherwise, they suffer from the phenomena of "group think," in which the group limits its thinking to the topics which hit the table first. After your staff has had an opportunity to perform their own SWOT analysis, gather their ideas and construct a master list of all issues. This may well bring some new matters to your attention that you haven't been aware of or have chosen to ignore. This list now becomes the basis for your strategic planning. Remember, this is not about ego; it is about reality, because the business can only operate in the realm of reality.

This list now becomes the basis for your further strategic planning. Inspect each of the Strengths, Weaknesses, Opportunities, and Threats, and determine what each of them implies for your own operation. There is no substitute for your own efforts, and so no passing this task along to someone else in the company. Here, the secret of success is in the details, and your own hard work. Good luck!

Run your business – don't let it run you. Common Sense.

SWOT Analysis Worksheet

INTERNAL	EXTERNAL
Strengths	**Opportunities**
➤ Key competencies / skill levels	➤ Skills transferable to new products/business
➤ Market reputation	➤ Product revision/update meets new demand
➤ Financial resource levels	➤ Customer demand levels increasing
➤ Economies of scale	➤ New technologies create more opportunities
➤ Production innovation	➤ Expanded vertical market channels
➤ Cost advantages	➤ Expanded horizontal market channels
➤ Relative experience	➤ Global sales opportunities
➤ Proven management	➤ Changes in tax structures
➤ Competitive Advantage	➤ Increased demand / increased capacity
➤ Expanding market penetration	➤ Competitive environment changing
➤ Talented personnel	➤ Rival business experiencing problems
➤ Established industry network	➤ Strategic partnering for increased sales
➤ Strong cross-channel relationships	➤ Proven e-commerce market demand
_____	_____
_____	_____
_____	_____
_____	_____
_____	_____
_____	_____
_____	_____
_____	_____
Weaknesses	**Threats**
➤ No strategic plan	➤ Increased competition
➤ Poor financial condition	➤ Declining demand
➤ Inadequate management skills	➤ Introduction of substitute product
➤ Understaffed or overstaffed	➤ Adverse trade policies
➤ Insufficient market strategy	➤ New trade regulations
➤ Wrong combination of personnel skills	➤ Strike in workforce
➤ Decreasing profitability	➤ Economic downturn or recession
➤ Obsolete resources	➤ Changing market demand
➤ Inadequate knowledge systems	➤ Demographic fluctuations
➤ Outdated product line	➤ Increased customer bargaining power
➤ Limited distribution network	➤ Increased supplier costs
➤ Poor market reputation	➤ International currency fluctuations
➤ Disjointed marketing strategy	➤ Competitor attracting away employees
➤ Stale management	➤ Untrained employment pool
_____	_____
_____	_____
_____	_____
_____	_____
_____	_____
_____	_____
_____	_____
_____	_____

Strategic Mapping Worksheet

STRATEGIC MAPPING						
				Projected & Actual Results		
	3 Year Goal	2 Year Goal	1 Year Goal	Present Year	Past Year	Past 2 Years
Sales						
Gross Margin						
Net Profit (EBIT)						
Breakeven						
Inventory						
Units Produced						
Units Sold						
Number of Customers						
Advertising Budget (% of Sales)						
Number of Employees						
Number of Locations						
(Place a checkmark for the following where applicable)						
Geographic Penetration						
Local						
Regional						
National						
International						
Internet Presence						
Website						
E-Commerce Site						
Other Factors						

Information Mapping

Strategic Planning Category	Measurement Criteria	Source of Data	Evaluation Criteria	Required Action
P&L Plan (Budget)	Target Costs / Revenues, Target Ratios	Accounting System	Deviations from Benchmarks	
Cash Flow Plan	Target Revenues, Target Expenses	Accounting System	Deviations from Budget Categories	
Organization al Mapping	Functional Time Use Analysis	Human Resources	Task Sheet Logs Maintained / Reviewed	
Time / Use Budget	Employee Work Performance	Weekly Work Plan	Deviations from Project Target Deadlines	
Financing Plan	Achievement of Target Goals	Accounting System	Strategic Analysis	
Inventory Plan	Adequacy of Inventory	Inventory Control System	Stock-outs / Cost Budget	
Advertising / Marketing Plan	Sales Volume, Growth	Accounting System	Deviations from Forecast	
AR / AP Forecast	Age of A/R Age of A/P	Accounting System	Deviations from Forecast	
Developmen t Plan	Meeting Time Goals	Various	PERT / CPM Other Tracking Systems	
Other				

© Knowledge Institute, Inc.

Dr. William R. Osgood
Cofounder, Knowledge Institute

Dr. William Osgood is recognized as one of the world's leading experts in entrepreneurial education and small business development. As an award-winning author, scholar and practitioner in the field of entrepreneurship, he has contributed to the success of millions of ventures, written dozens of business management books, launched a number of entrepreneurial ventures and consulted with numerous organizations on issues dealing with venture creation, finance and high growth strategies. His books have been published in multiple languages, distributed internationally, and are used by academic institutions, government, economic development agencies and private consulting firms in fostering and teaching entrepreneurship.

As an innovator of entrepreneurial learning systems, he authored the first interactive Business Planning Guide; developed BIC-NET as the first public/private small business resource network, which became the U.S. Small Business Administration's national Business Information Center (BIC) network; and defined a *Systems Approach to Venture Initiation,* which has been praised in academic journals. His knowledge in effectively driving small business start-up and economic growth has been sought after by leading private sector and government organizations including Microsoft, IBM, The World Bank, Bank of America, Verizon, American Express, U.S. Department of Labor, U.S. Department of Education and State Economic Development Agencies.

Known as Dr. Bill to many, he has taught and guest lectured at numerous colleges and universities including Harvard University, Massachusetts Institute of Technology and Babson College, and has been a featured guest in television, radio and social media including WCVB-TV, WMUR-TV and Comcast Newsmakers. The U.S. Small Business Administration (SBA) recognizes Dr. Bill as a small business development expert and named him Small Business Advocate of the Year.

Ahead of his time, Dr. Bill's signature approach to entrepreneurial education is combining multimedia platforms to provide step-by-step, interactive learning systems. Through a series of steps, interactive exercises, plug-and-play templates and customizable worksheets, skills are developed incrementally and immediately applied to real world business situations across the learning continuum. Dr. Bill refers to this educational technique as *Business Knowledgement*™; just in time learning with immediate application to contemporary business management challenges.

His small business development proficiency stems from his early career as manager of urban affairs at the Federal Reserve Bank of Boston where he developed a program for providing subsidized business planning and management support to growing small business ventures, authored the *New England Business Resource Directory*, and taught undergraduate and graduate courses in entrepreneurship at Northeastern University, University of New Hampshire, Southern New Hampshire University, Boston University, College for Lifelong Learning and University of New Hampshire.

Dr. Bill holds a Doctorate in System Development and Adaptation from Boston University with a concentration in Organizational Behavior, graduating summa cum laude; a Masters in Business Administration from Northeastern University, and a Bachelor of Business Science from Southern New Hampshire University. He is a strong civic leader and a United States Veteran.

He may be reached at the Knowledge Institute, Inc., 11 Court Street, Suite 230, Exeter, NH 03833; by phone at (603) 658-0340; or by email at wro@bdki.com.

www.ingramcontent.com/pod-product-compliance
Lightning Source LLC
Chambersburg PA
CBHW060401220326
41598CB00023B/2991